Health and Medicine
in the Anglican Tradition

Health/Medicine and the Faith Traditions

Edited by Martin E. Marty and Kenneth L. Vaux

Health/Medicine and the Faith Traditions
explores the ways in which major religions
relate to the questions of human well-being.
It issues from Project Ten, an interfaith program
of The Park Ridge Center, An Institute for the Study of
Health, Faith, and Ethics.

James P. Wind, Director of Research and Publications

The Park Ridge Center,
a Division of the Lutheran Institute of Human Ecology,
is part of the Lutheran General Health Care System,
in Park Ridge, Illinois.

Health and Medicine in the Anglican Tradition

Conscience, Community, and Compromise

David H. Smith

Crossroad · New York

1986
The Crossroad Publishing Company
370 Lexington Ave, New York, N.Y. 10017

Library of Congress Cataloging in Publication Data

Smith, David H., 1939–
Health and medicine in the Anglican tradition.

(Health/medicine and the faith traditions)
1. Health—Religious aspects—Anglican Communion.
2. Medicine—Religious aspcts—Anglican Communion.
3. Anglican Communion—Doctrines. I. Title.
II. Series. [DNLM]: 1. Christianity. 2. Ethics,
Medical. 3. Religion and Medicine. W 50 S645h]
BX5008.9.H42S65 1986   241'.642   85–29937
ISBN 0–8245–0716–9

For
Celeste R. and Herbert L. Smith
and in memory of
Martha L. and Leonard E. Arnaud

Contents

Foreword

The Anglican Communion numbers about 50 million people in 165 countries. The *World Christian Encyclopedia* regards it as one of seven major blocs in Christendom, alongside Catholicism, Orthodoxy, "Non-White Indigenous," "Marginal Protestant," "Catholic (Non-Roman)" and "Protestant." It is in this latter category that most Americans locate their Anglican or, as they usually call them, Episcopal neighbors. There are 2,767,440 of these in the *Yearbook of American and Canadian Churches* in the year of this writing. They frequent 7,234 churches or local congregations. That means that in all but those 7,234 communities Anglicanism may seem remote, alien; it might as well be "Marginal Protestant," so far as citizens in, say, overwhelmingly Southern Baptist, Jewish, Norwegian Lutheran, or Italian Catholic communities are concerned.

Were Professor Smith writing for and about only those Episcopal Church members, his book would still have great potential and validity. These millions of people have somehow situated themselves where many human, religious, and Christian meanings are prismed through the Anglican experience. Not many of them are conscious of the distinctive ways Anglican thinkers and actors have addressed questions of health and well-being. As is the case with so many books in this series, Smith's is the first within his faith community to deal specifically with the juncture of the religious tradition and the search for human care, healing, and meaning in the face of suffering. That is not to say that no works have made comment. Smith would have little to talk about were there not inherited texts like those of Jeremy Taylor to which he so regularly returns. Yet such texts have not been synoptic or synthetic. They have been expressions of pastoral or therapeutic concern by Anglicans to people in specific time, place, and situation. Smith, as it were, sits Jeremy Taylor and Richard Hooker and (the younger) Joseph Fletcher around the table and produces a sort of conversation that draws upon their work and that of others.

Eavesdroppers on that conversation, listeners-in from the nation's or the world's overwhelmingly non-Anglican majority, will make several kinds of uses of what they read here. A minimal response would be to say something like, "I never knew that before," or "I didn't know that Anglicanism had much to say on these subjects," or "Didn't Smith do well to dredge this up and display it so well?" A second level of response will be comparative: one learns about his or her own tradition by comparing it with those that run alongside it, nearby or at distant range. Third, a book like this goes a long way to explain some of the attitudes behind health care and understandings in the English-speaking West. There, because of its privileged social location, Anglicanism has had influence far beyond its numbers. I can picture beyond this aid to understanding key aspects of the Anglo-American world two additional kinds of uses, one by which Anglicans would blend elements of their own theory and practice with those from other faiths and another that would lead non-Anglicans to adopt elements from this tradition, where congenial, and make them their own. This goes on all the time in the worlds of theory and therapy, and Smith makes such goings-on easy, so clearly does he isolate Anglican themes.

Let me pause for a moment and comment on the second of these levels, comparison, It may seem bad manners for the author of one book in the series to refer to his own when writing forewords to others, but the illustration will, I believe, redeem me from charges of committing gaucheries. After I had written on the Lutheran tradition, which in this series lies cheek by jowl alongside both the Reformed and the Anglican—too close, some might think, to justify all these nuanced volumes!—I had a conversation with a Roman Catholic medical professional. "You Lutherans surely are word-centered, aren't you!" was his summary. "I can't get over how much faith you have in preaching, in speech, when you encounter illness or would be well. Words and the Word—that's what it all seems to be about."

While I may wish to refine or add to that analysis, I could not and would not evade its main thrust. This was the case even though I, as a Lutheran and a student of Lutheranism, did not even recognize this while writing the book. Now. as I read David Smith's book, the "word-centeredness" of Lutheranism stood in ever more bold relief against the Anglican approach. Not that Anglicanism does not care for words. After all, it gave the English-speaking world the King James Version of the Bible, the *Book of Common Prayer*, and authors from John Donne through T. S. Eliot and W. H. Auden and C. S. Lewis. Its preachers preach and its prayers pray with verbal force and eloquence. Anglicans tell stories to those who are ill and proclaim prophetically when injustice stands in the way of health care. Words count, and they count for very much.

All that having been said, however, it is clear from Smith's pages that other elements of transaction between God and humans are equally stressed. Thus we learn that there is not ordinarily the preaching of the word at the burial of the dead. Other aspects of care come into play. It is clear that here is a tradition that underplays "crisis" theology, "dialectical" thinking, apocalypticism—though it has bred some apocalyptic spin-offs. Instead Anglicanism stresses the divine act of creation. Where others accept the atonement in Jesus Christ, Anglicans affirm it and then move to the incarnation. To them, the affirmation that the Divine Creator revisits creation, is bonded with it and its destiny, in the figure of Jesus Christ, is a better base for interpreting the body, suffering, and hope. Anglicans make many such conscious choices, and Smith does well to point them out.

The Episcopalian down the block may never have read Richard Hooker or Jeremy Taylor, and may not be moved to start doing so now. There is no sectarian interest on these pages. Smith is not suggesting that the world will come to healing or produce better care if everyone turns Anglican, joins the club, and takes signals from that. Such a suggestion would be very un-Anglican, for this is an ecumenical tradition and one that has built "comprehension" of diversities into its heart. He does not have to suggest, he demonstrates, that the Anglican tradition has riches for those in it and for those who take pains to come into the zones where it is active.

I used the Lutheran comparison above to isolate some Anglican motifs in anticipation of Smith's pages. Other readers will do their own comparing. They are likely to find that if one wishes to come across the Anglican heart, the place to find it is not in the theology classroom, on the evangelistic circuit, or the lobbies of legislatures. That heart beats best at the eucharist, at worship, where believers commune with God in Christ and with each other. It is just as clear that from such a central act they derive meanings that have influence often unrecognized on how they face death, determine the ethics of generation, the ways of sexual being, and the responsibilities for justice in the delivery of health services.

Anglicanism often looks relaxed to more fervent bystanders and observers. Episcopalians may be charismatic—a "Spirit" movement prospers among them and has much to say about healing—but most of them seem to share sacred space in quiet, almost diffident ways. They may be zealous about the condition of the Prayer Book and the status of Apostolic Succession, but they do not try to get in other people's way. Yet they are to be encountered wherever people think deeply about theology and health and ethics. They take responsibility for the life of their communities, including its health care facilities. They do not build high walls around themselves;

that is why observers often overlook the center around which they are drawn. It is Smith's effort, one that appears to be very successful, to examine that center and to make it available to those drawn to it magnetically, as Anglicans themselves, or as those who have been barely conscious that it exists.

MARTIN E. MARTY
University of Chicago

"It is not morally eligible for the moralist to enunciate a formula which, however orthodox and conclusive it may appear to him, is yet demonstrably beyond the capacity of most of the people whom he would require to live by it."

— Board for Social Responsibility (Church of England), *Sterilization: An Ethical Inquiry*

"When and if it becomes possible to control the sex of unborn children, we will no doubt breed a generation of hermaphrodites for fear of committing our children to an identity and a fate not of their own choosing."

— Everett Hughes, *Cycles and Turning Points*

Preface

No one can be all things to all people, and no book can serve all possible purposes. There are three things this book is not: First, it is not a survey of various Anglican views on questions of health and disease, morals and mortality, the communication and community of life. It is not even a survey of *recent* Anglican statements on those subjects, for the important Warnock Commission Report and the related literature have been too recent for serious discussion here. A thorough historical book is needed; Dean John Booty[1] of Sewanee has made a thought-provoking start on what it might involve, and the writing task calls for a historical scholar. I do not want to claim that the essay I offer here is better than or a substitute for that kind of book.

Secondly, despite the form of the first chapters, I do not claim to have stated the essence of Anglicanism from which other views depart only by splitting off from the family tradition. In fact I think it essential to Anglicanism to resist any such clear statement of its essence. The first steps in understanding this tradition are historical and political rather than metaphysical. And thirdly, the book is not meant to be a weighty tome, but —like other books in the Health/Medicine and the Faith Traditions series —it is designed for health professionals, clergy, and others seriously struggling with issues of religion and medicine.

What, then, is this book meant to be? An essay, identifiably Anglican, that addresses the issues raised by thoughtful persons and focused in the themes of this series. It is meant to be a characteristically Anglican argument. I sketch what that means in the first chapters and attempt to fill out the themes as I go along. Furthermore, a major part in the dialogue is played by Anglican writers who have addressed the questions I take up. Even here I make no claim to comprehensive coverage, but I hope I touch some major bases, for I am trying to make a case that Anglican churches should hold to the conclusions I argue for. This book does advance a set of normative proposals, whatever their weaknesses.

Anglican authors, however, are not my only conversation partners. It will be clear to many readers that my perspective is formed not just by the community in which I have worshiped throughout my life, but by the characteristically American theology of H. Richard Niebuhr, his forefathers like Josiah Royce, and his intellectual progeny: Paul Ramsey, James Gustafson and William F. May. Thus this is self-consciously an *American* Anglican book, although I think it has relevance for other places and histories. I make no apology for this characteristic of the book; indeed I offer a theological justification for it in the first chapter, and I am convinced that it is important to attempt a synthesis between English Anglican and American theological writers.

It remains for me to acknowledge some of my debts. The first of these is to Kenneth Vaux and David Stein, who entrusted this book to me at a time when I needed to ask for time and who have provided generous support throughout its gestation.

Research for the volume really began in 1980 during six months spent in England through the generous support of a Lilly Open Fellowship. I am most grateful to the Lilly Endowment and its then vice-president for education, Dr. Laura Bornholdt, for making that year possible. During that six months I enjoyed warm hospitality and provocative conversation from many persons, notably Basil Mitchell, David Jenkins, Gordon Dunstan, Maurice Wiles and Ian Thompson. My introduction to English medical practice was largely through the good offices of Robert Twycross and his colleagues, especially Ms. Gwenyth Lowe at Sir Michael Sobell House, where I had the remarkable privilege of working as a volunteer. Robert Edwards gave me an invaluable primer on the work of an English G.P.— and in most hospitable circumstances. Edward Shotter in London and Kenneth Boyd in Edinburgh could not have been more generous or open with the resources of the Medical Groups. If the book that follows shows any feel at all for Anglicanism beyond my own national experience, these are the people I have to thank.

More recently an earlier, and longer, version of chapters 1–4 was given a fair reading and serious critique by Luke Johnson, the Rev. Hugh Laughlin, John Pless, M.D., and the Rev. Joseph Rautenberg. It was an act of friendship and fraternal correction I shall not forget. Earlier my thoughts on care of the dying were enriched, as was my life, by contact with Dr. William Elliott, Sr. And subsequently Elof Axel Carlson, Gilbert Meilaender, and Henry Veatch subjected the manuscript to characteristically good-hearted and rigorous criticism. Finally, I should report that my work on this project has been invaluably assisted by Ms. Judith Granbois and Ms. Beverly Davis, who have seen it through more stages and prevented more errors than I can count. None of its limits are due to any of these friends, of course.

· 1 ·

Anglicanism

What Anglicans Are

One possible definition of Anglicanism is simply the Established Church in England and its descendants in the sometime British colonies. The denomination is not united by the thought of one great thinker, or even by an extensive set of counciliar or creedal statements. Thus on more than one occasion when I have discussed this book with friends, including clergy, I have been met with raised eyebrows and shrugged shoulders. Perhaps naïvely I have construed these responses as signs of despair when forced to deal with the question of what Anglicanism says about anything. For the only chorus that responds is polyphonal.

This ideological cacophony does not mean, however, that the tradition lacks an identity. I think that there are characteristically Anglican perspectives on some matters central to the themes of this book: on suffering and human dignity, on community and health, on morality, conventions and the natural. In this first chapter I shall state these perspectives as best I can, hoping to lay a foundation for the more specific discussion of issues that follows. I shall not attempt a comprehensive statement of Anglicanism, and even what I do will be fragmentary. My objective is to underscore certain themes in the tradition.

The most basic of these is a conviction about reality, the idea that the fundamental power, God, has identified himself with humankind in the person and mission of Jesus. Naturally this claim raises many difficult conceptual issues about both God and Jesus. Great and ongoing discussions of the doctrine of the Trinity and of Christology have informed and continue to excite the Anglican communion, and this is not the place—nor am I the person—to attempt to resolve them. But it is important to see that Anglicanism begins with a distinctively theological affirmation, however much interpretations of it may differ. This affirmation involves three subordinate themes, all important to the basic subject matter of this book: suffering, human nature and community.

Suffering

Anglicanism has generally held that reconciliation between humankind and God is made necessary by the misery and unhappiness of human existence. If human persons were not alienated, alone, sick and starving—if human existence were not in some way deficient—then there would be nothing to be gained from communion with God. But because people suffer in body and mind improvement is possible. Thus this tradition begins with a realistic assessment of the human prospect. Life may not always be "nasty, brutish and short," but it invariably involves suffering.

Nowhere is this reality more clear than in institutions and careers committed to health care. The following narrative is one of many that could be taken from *The New England Journal of Medicine* in an article that was published more than ten years ago.

> Baby B was referred to . . . [the MD] at the age of 36 hours with duodenal obstruction and signs of Down's syndrome. His young parents had a ten-year-old daughter, and he was the son they had been trying to have for ten years; yet, when they were approached with the operative consent, they hesitated. They wanted to know beyond any doubt whether the baby had Down's syndrome. If so, they wanted time to consider whether or not to permit the surgery to be done. Within 8 hours a geneticist was able to identify cells containing 47 chromosomes in a bone-marrow sample. Over the next three days the infant's gastrointestinal tract was decompressed with a nasogastric tube, and he was supported with intravenous fluids while the parents consulted with their ministers, with family physicians in their home community, and with our geneticists. At the end of that time, the B's decided not to permit surgery. The infant died three days later after the withdrawal of supportive therapy.[1]

Not only babies and parents suffer:

> She is a 55-year-old woman who was lying in a dimly lit dilapidated apartment when we first met her. Her room was filled with pails of vomitus; newpapers placed around the room were soaked with diarrhea and vomitus. She had been ill for six days, but refused to be carried to D.C. General because she feared she would die. Beside her immediate health problems, she had a large mass below her breast which was draining; chronic back pain with two collapsed vertebrae in her back; marked weakness in her hand, secondary to an old injury which made it difficult for her to grasp or hold objects. Over the past several years her life had been spent taking care of a dying man who lived next door, a job which required heavy lifting, and a job which she had taken in order to pay for rent and food. She had now given up and turned to alcohol. Eventually, through trust, she entered an outpatient alcoholism program and Voca-

tional Rehabilitation. During this time she applied for welfare, her only source of income which is $180/month. Although she was declared to be unable to work by Vocational Rehabilitation, she was refused SSI payments because she was not totally disabled.[2]

To be sure, some of these problems have been created for us by the remarkable successes of twentieth-century medicine, but this should not blind us to the fact that ultimately all medicine is palliative, engaged in patching, renewing and perhaps some redesigning of mortal flesh. The brokenness of life—of healer and patient—is there for anyone with eyes to see.

The Anglican tradition insists that in Jesus God was identified with this brokenness and suffering. God shares in the suffering. Thus it is an academic's mistake to ask, "How could a good God allow this to happen?"—for the central Anglican affirmation about God in Christ is that he has owned suffering for himself by undergoing it. In Christian experience the identification of God with suffering humankind precedes and therefore may qualify (although I think it need not contradict) belief in the omnipotence of God.

David Jenkins, the bishop of Durham, made the point in *The Glory of Man*. In Jesus, he writes, there is "a personal union between transcendent personalness, and derived personalness," a union that suggests a redefinition of the power of God as "self-giving, identifying and involved love."[3] The actual portrait of Jesus, from which Christianity began, is an actuality of "suffering, dying and forsakenness. . . . The pattern which gives shape to the universe . . . is lived out in materiality and history as a man who succumbs to suffering and evil."

Explanation of suffering and evil are beyond our grasp, Jenkins suggests, "but we do see that the human being who embodies the pattern of the loving God is both submerged in the destruction of evil and emerges from it as a distinctive, living and personal activity. The Logos of the cosmos is not a mythological theory but a crucified man."[4] The suffering of *God* in Christ must be acknowledged.[5]

Thus one part of the Anglican response to suffering is to affirm that the sufferer is not alone. Without anticipating the rest of the book, we can say that this perspective has some clear implications for medicine. First is the conviction of the inevitability of suffering. This is not the same thing as advocating suffering, although I shall approach that idea later. But if suffering is really inevitable, this fact suggests a limit to possible medical progress. To be sure we may change the forms of suffering people experience, but not the fact. Therefore, to equate the goal of medicine with the elimination of suffering is mistaken. We should distinguish *health*—an appropriate limited and limiting goal of medicine—from some more comprehensive term such as *wholeness*, which is sought by both medical and religious communities. A Promethean vision of medical possibilities is ill-suited to an Anglican sensibility.

Second, the salvation that is made possible by the incarnation does not fundamentally consist of bringing suffering to an end. Rather, salvation involves God's participation in suffering, to establish community between suffering humankind and himself. Salvation does not mean an end to suffering; it means an end to *isolated* suffering. So far as we can tell, suffering will continue forever. "The Son of God suffered unto death, not that men might not suffer, but that their sufferings might be like his."[6]

Robert Lambourne may have seen this point more clearly, and pushed it further, than any other recent Anglican writer. He insisted that Jesus offered healing to body and spirit by identifying himself with those who were sick. When Jesus, the representative person, joins himself to another in healing, suffering does not disappear, but it is transformed. The community that continues this process suffers in its identification with suffering persons; the wholeness it creates is honest, for it is "a wholeness which includes suffering."

> Those modern and ancient Gnostics who see perfect faith in Christ as necessitating perfect freedom from suffering must not only set aside the bloody and exhausted Christ on the cross, but Christ's repeated statements that faith in him means sharing in his suffering. . . . He who would share his life must lose it. He who would be made whole must suffer as he joins the suffering of man in Christ.[7]

So where is the good news in the midst of all this? It begins with the creation of community. A sick person who is identified with God and others is reconciled with them and enabled to love. Lambourne's points are that incarnational Christianity requires direct involvement in healing of bodies, and that the ultimate healing or "perfect wholeness" offered by Christ and church is the creation of community through honest acceptance and exchange of suffering. Cicely Saunders puts it well: "We find in grief not only that we belong with all other men but that we belong with God also. We, and those we love, wherever we may be, are safe."[8]

These considerations are essential in Anglican reflection about health and disease, medicine and theology. The tradition or perspective does not begin with individual rights, with an ideal of self-determination or hope for physical perfection. Nor does it expect or believe in an end to or escape from suffering. Its assessments of the human self and anticipated rewards are more modest.

Human Nature and Dignity

I have said that suffering is the human lot, but God's identification with persons opens new possibilities. These include a new sense of human worth and dignity that derives from the special involvement of God with persons. The core idea is *adoption*. As Jesus is confessed to be the Son of God, so the Christian is thought to be, in the words of the Apostle Paul, an adopted son. The ritual context in which this relationship is declared to be a reality is baptism, a kind of symbolic reiteration by the Christian of Jesus' death and resurrection. The Christian's involvement with God is derivative from the exemplary and first-person involvement of Christ, but it remains involvement all the same. An adopted child is a real child of the parents.

According to Richard Hooker, the sixteenth-century defender of Anglicanism, the adoption is central in baptism—a ritual process Hooker thought was instituted "that they which receive the same might thereby be incorporated into Christ."[9] The process is continued in the eucharist. Christ is our life, Hooker writes, "because through him we obtain life." The bread and wine of the sacrament are called body and blood because they are "causes instrumental" of "our participation of his body and blood."[10] The elements, he thinks, are not and do not really contain grace, for the human self rather than the elements "is the receptacle of Christ's presence."[11] For Hooker and the subsequent Anglican tradition the rituals attest an identification between individual Christians and God incarnate in Christ. Recognition of this community is much more important than specific theoretical explanations of *how* identification is established.[12]

The result, according to Hooker, is to establish a relationship of "participation," which is "that mutual inward hold which Christ hath of us and we of him, in such sort that each possesses other by way of special interest, property and inherent copulation."[13] God is in all things as creator and sustainer, he continues, but persons receive "the gracious and amiable name of sons" and are "in God." "By virtue of this mystical conjunction, we are of him and in him even as though our very flesh and bones should be made continuate with his."

We become "coherent" with God,[14] and the effects are felt in our very bodies.[15] Hooker says that God has "deified our nature, though not by turning it into himself, yet by making it his own inseparable habitation." Therefore, "we cannot now conceive how God should without man either exercise divine power or receive the glory of divine praise. For man is in both an associate of Deity."[16]

Thus Anglicanism has tended to suggest that the core of human dignity lies in relationship to God rather than in qualities of intelligence or free will. It is, as the Lutheran theologian Helmut Thielicke once put it, an "alien dignity" in the sense that it is the property of a relationship rather than of human nature in itself as such. Salvation is found in true community; damnation is isolation; sin involves the pretense of radical independence.

The relational theme was central for J. F. D. Maurice, a nineteenth-century Anglican theologian and social reformer. We can regard someone from either of two points of view, he suggested: as an object that can be seen and handled, or as a son, or a brother, a daughter or sister. Thought of as an object, a person lives in material circumstances,

> but that which is necessary in an account of myself, seems to be entitled to another name. We commonly call it a relationship. . . . We speak of a man *having* a bad disposition or bad hearing; we speak of his *being* a bad brother or a bad son.[17]

To be a self is to be in relationship, but relationship is not limited to families. Persons are meant for larger and better bonds, e.g., in national communities. The self is a member of many communities; it is constituted by multifarious loyalties. "[H]uman relationships are not artificial types of something divine, but are actually means and the only means, through which man ascends to any knowledge of the divine. . . ."[18]

There are important medical implications of this relational anthropology. Negatively it suggests that Anglicanism will be uncomfortable with what we might call ontological simplification in medical decision-making. Many dilemmas encountered at both the beginning and end of life could be removed if we could hold that certain classes of humans—embryos, fetuses, infants, the retarded, the senile or the decerebrate—lack the essential components of human dignity and could, therefore, be discounted. This kind of simplifying strategy makes sense if human dignity is a function of some nonrelational property, such as intelligence. But that reasoning is less plausible when human dignity is derivative; at the very least it would be hard for Anglicans to hold that a being who might be baptized was lacking in human dignity.

Positively this notion of human life as a life incorporated into God's life suggests a self-consciousness that is nonservile and able to live in hope. It is not possible to generalize about Anglican views on an afterlife, but it is important to see that adoption means communion with a power more fundamental than death or, otherwise expressed, eternal life. Some believe that eternal life includes personal resurrection or immortality; for all it suggests hope in the ultimate acceptance of the self. Derivative children of the Father live in "the sure and certain hope of the resurrection."

This kind of stance is not just "positive thinking" for it proceeds from a sense of the inevitability of suffering, and it is a life of hope rather than of *self*-confidence. But it does suggest something about the dignity of the self that complements my first, negative point. A child of God, living in hope, is nothing to be trifled with. Its self, judgments and fate matter; it is appropriate to be *indignant* when they are not taken seriously. Consistent with this conclusion, Anglicanism has wanted to make the informed conscience of the individual into a sacred court of appeal. Children of God must make up their own minds. Thus if situationalism is mistaken—as I think it to be—it is a characteristically Anglican form of theological mistake, originating in a firm grasp of a truth: If I have been brought into contact with eternal life, I am responsible for thinking about the requirements of that life. Kenneth Kirk, the twentieth-century Anglican moralist and bishop of Oxford wrote:

> If . . . [someone] has her [the church's] welfare at heart he must play his part in the process of selecting from among a vast number of competing practices and opinions that dominate laws and customs of the future. . . . Only as members of the church set themselves to play their part in the framing of custom in a responsible and intelligent fashion, have we any right to suppose that they are fully cooperating with the Holy Spirit in the task of keeping the church's ethical system aligned with the self-revealing will of God for man.[19]

Kirk put the idea well. Persons have a duty not just to themselves but to God and the church, to reason a problem through.

Community

The affirmations just mentioned naturally involve another: that human selves are fundamentally social and exist in community with one another.

Our true nature is as selves who are, as Hooker put it, "sociable parts united into one body," according to a natural law that binds us "each to serve unto other's good, and all to prefer the good of the whole before whatsoever their own particular."[20] The source of this "sociable communion" is "a natural delight which man hath to transfuse from himself into others and to receive from others into himself especially those things wherein the excellence of his kind doth most consist."[21] Hooker's image of the self is of a social self, saved in relationship to Christ, required to grow in that relationship and in community. The seventeenth-century Anglican casuist Robert Sanderson put the point well:

> God hath made us sociable creatures, contrived us into policies and societies and commonwealths; made us fellow members of one body and every one another's members. As, therefore, we are not born, so neither must we live, to and for ourselves alone; but our parents and friends, and acquaintances, nay, every man of us hath a kind of right and interest in every other man of us, and our country and the commonwealth in us all.[22]

As I have suggested, this community is established in ritual or worship. Indeed some observers claim that Anglicanism is held together more by a common attitude toward ritual than by anything else. To start with, ritual represents or reiterates actions central to the memory of the community. This process of recollection is most clear in baptism and the eucharist, which involve dramatic representations of Jesus's death and resurrection, representations that are done and owned by the community. But other rituals— of confirmation, marriage, ordination or burial—also involve remembering past acts of great significance.

Rituals also signal several kinds of transitions. Some are seasonal; others, as those just named, pertain to the individual life cycle. The *rites de passage* of traditional societies mark stages on a life's way. They were not related to trivia but made public an acknowledgment of real changes in life. A ritual may, like marriage, cause a change to occur or, like a funeral, it may be an acknowledgment that something has happened. But good ritual will always have two characteristics. First, it is honest, cutting through denial and forcing a realization about change. As Everett Hughes once wrote: "[S]o long as the rites are practiced there is no attempt to deny the realities of the human life cycle."[23]

Secondly, rituals always involve human relations of association and disassociation. That is, they relate to commitments that individuals make, to loyalties that they cannot help but acquire. It may not be coincidental, as Hughes points out, that Americans are deficient both in public ritual and in recognition about commitment.

> We no longer like to take vows; that is to make commitments for ourselves . . . [or] for others, even our own children. And in all rites of initiation or

transition there is commitment either for oneself or for someone else, or for both. [But] . . . we are unwilling to commit ourselves and even more unwilling to commit our children to anything, even to a social identity.[24]

The public acknowledgment of a change of status means cutting oneself off from some things (pagan gods, possible spouses, or the life of a layman) and involving oneself in others (the triune God, one's spouse, the priesthood). These are not merely external changes; they affect the very being of the self. Thus, gradual as they may sometimes seem, these changes inevitably involve or commit the self to new relations, roles and duties. Ritual is both a creator and a product of ongoing ties of fidelity.

Ritual performs this community-creating role by reminding us of the past, for it bridges a gap between past and present. Worship involves a remembering or making present of past events of exodus or crucifixion and, through the representation, renewing the community's identity. Individually and collectively we inevitably understand or interpret ourselves with reference to our past. If I ask who I am, I must begin to answer the question in terms of my past history, for any novelty I may have consists of a blending or qualification of what the philosopher Josiah Royce once called these "streams of ancestral tendency."

In other words, ritual makes clear we are parts of a tradition, of ideas and loyalties that have been handed over and reinterpreted over time. Ritual consciousness always wants to relate to, or interpret, the past. Thus Hooker thought it a mistake to depart unnecessarily from established practice, for people and societies learn by experience. He quotes Aristotle to the effect that judgments of experienced men are like proofs.[25] Acts of a community done five hundred years ago "standeth as theirs who presently are of the same societies, because corporations are immortal; we were then alive in our predecessors, and they in their successors do live still."[26]

Traditions cannot give "specific solutions to new problems," but they yield "a variety of principles of general application." These are the words of the contemporary Anglican moralist Gordon Dunstan. Traditional principles, he contends, are data to be used or reasoned with. The reasoning process is not "a process of logical deduction from a stated principle to a particular application"; rather, a sense of fitness points to a certain conclusion" that is "not contrary to the moral tradition, or may . . . exemplify it in a way that, though new, is more of a fulfillment than any other possibility open at the time."[27]

Kenneth Kirk put the point this way:

> Conscience is not a discoverer of the unknown, but a craftsman working upon the known; and it is folly in a craftsman to jettison the tools or the materials with which he has been provided merely because he has not yet been able to find a use for them.... We receive from society not merely the traditions we criticise, but the canons of criticism which we apply to them, and it is ungrateful and unfair to accept the one gift and spurn the other before we have made every effort to find out whether both ... cannot be held together in the same system.[28]

Rituals serve to establish community among persons both in social space and over time—with the children of God in the past and with those who are to come. Identity of self or community is a product of history and tradition, cannot be understood apart from it, and provides guidelines for reasoning about the future.

In a medical context these beliefs at least imply that it is impossible to respect the dignity of a self in abstraction from the communities of which it is a part or from the history and hopes that inform its life. Individuality is a product of social relations and history; and medical "histories" or bases for decision-making that leave this dimension out of account omit central details in the pursuit of health.

Morals

Because it perceives the world in the way I have just described, Anglicanism is mightily concerned with morals. From Joseph Butler in the eighteenth century to R. M. Hare in this one, it has included among its members philosophical moralists of the first rank. Indeed some contend that there is a consistent Anglican strand of *moralism* going back to Pelagius in the fourth century. Pelagius seemed to say that persons can find salvation on their own, if only they will work hard enough. This assertion provoked Augustine of Hippo to formulate his great doctrines of grace and free will, insisting that salvation is a gift from God rather than a possible human achievement. In this he persuaded not only continental Europe but the English church as well: The communion is not Pelagian.

But it is, and always has been, very concerned with human action and responsibility. The basis for this concern is the convictions about human nature and community that I sketched above, which involve realism, a rejection of fatalism and a heightened sense of responsibility. But there are three important components in Anglican reflection about morals that we should take up separately: fidelity or loyalty, convention and the natural.

Fidelity

The central Anglican moral principle is loyalty or fidelity to God and to other persons. Because I am a being who lives in relationships, I should act accordingly. Some other ideal or moral frame of reference will put me out of gear with the fundamental facts of the human world.

The fulfillment of the soul in relationship to God has always been taken seriously by Anglicanism. It has continued a tradition of the "cure of souls" from Reformation times, and there is a great tradition of Anglican mystics. Rich as this literature is, its major relevance for our immediate purpose is its clear presupposition that the self or person ultimately transcends the human community and finds its identity in a relationship of devotion to and trust in God. The model, of course, comes from the trust and struggles of Jesus with the power he called Father.

On the other hand, Jesus also provides a model of how God relates to persons and therefore of how we should relate to each other. If he illustrates passion for God, he also shows compassion for other persons[29] by caring for them, forgiving them and ministering to them in their physical and mental brokenness. Indeed we might say that Jesus died because of his realization that trust in God required this sort of commitment to humankind.

Because Anglicanism looks at the world and morals this way there is one kind of theme in medical ethics that it cannot embrace: the idea that, as Erich Fromm once put it, man is "for himself." The mistaken idea, not exactly Fromm's, is that persons are independent, social relations are contingent or external and that, therefore, a self's fate is simply its own business. I will return to this theme repeatedly. For the moment I wish only to make the general observation that the vision of selfhood it involves is more timid and shriven than the Anglican perspective. An uncommitted or uninvolved self is safe because it has reduced its vulnerabilities—the territory where its identity can be attacked—to a bare minimum. But if reality really is what the trinitarian confession claims—power committing itself to others and being crucified into the bargain—then true life for the self is found in owning involvements that are essential to its existence, and this "owning" can be expected to involve both death and resurrection.

A life of fidelity, in other words, is a life of *increased* vulnerability to suffering that comes from identifying oneself with other frail and broken persons. The enlarged sense of self and rooting in God's love mean this suffering is borne in hope. But no more than for Jesus in Gethsemane or on Golgotha is this an easy hope.

In the body of the book I shall spell out what seem to me to be some of the requirements of fidelity in a medical setting, but first two general comments about the Anglican understanding of this norm are in order.

Convention

The first derives from earlier remarks about the importance of community. Fidelity within Anglicanism is very concerned with "conventions," which are "means of giving stability and permanence to a moral insight," because "without the institution it [the insight] is likely to be lost in time of need."[30] Conventions have prescriptive force because they crystallize the expectations of the community; they embody "in institutional form what the community believes to be worthy."[31] They limit self-interest and excess compassion. Thus, in an important sense, conventions are liberating, for they provide the self with some predictability in the background before which it acts.[32] They are cultural habits, practices and traditions.

These conventions should be distinguished from civil law, passed by Congress or Parliament. The Anglican idea is that civil legislation is only one, and not the best, method of shaping and forming society. Thus, in the eighth book of the *Laws of Ecclesiastical Polity*, Hooker argued that communities or states, like persons, have both a "spiritual" and a "temporal" nature. Therefore, he concluded, societies require two sets of institutions.

Maurice made the incarnational basis of this viewpoint more explicit. Both our duty to love (learned in the New Testament) and our duty to hate enemies must be maintained, if love is not to become a "weak contemptible tolerance for that which is unlovely."[33] How to preserve both sets of duties? The answer is duality of social institutions—both church and nation. These two articulations of society provide a divine scheme "for upholding love in its fullness lest law should perish; for upholding law in its fullness lest love should perish. . . ."[34]

For Maurice and Hooker an essential dimension of Christian reflection begins with the traditions and institutions of the community in which one lives. Christian ideas about politics and society, health and disease, birth and death are not always and everywhere the same. Christian thought about these things cannot be a "system," by which Maurice meant a deductive set of moral propositions necessarily opposed to "life, freedom, variety."[35] Instead people need a "method" of work or investigation that he called "digging." Anglican reasoning goes wrong when its primary concerns are systems and consistency.

Because of its concerns with tradition and convention Anglicanism expects the reasonable choice to be, to a degree, a function of time and place. Moral epistemology is historical; the loyal thing to do is not something that can be deduced once and for all. Egil Grislis quotes Hooker: "Two things there are which trouble greatly these later times: one, that the Church of Rome cannot, another that Geneva will not erre." Against these dogmatisms Hooker thought truth was hard to come by. "There simply is [for Hooker] no theological method, however correct, that can itself ensure its own infallibility."[36] Wisdom, therefore, comes from "whole nations living through centuries" with the best thinkers of the community's past.[37] Inconsistencies will naturally occur, but this is "the admission of inconsistencies inherent in life itself, and of the impossibility of overcoming them by the imposition of a uniformity greater than life will bear."[38] Anglicanism "has taken the course of reducing the domain of law to the barest possible minimum . . . leaving all else to the regime of custom."[39]

Thus in envisioning the world of the hospital or figuring out how to cope with problems, it is appropriate to begin with perspectives and customs that are to be found there. A perspective of fidelity does not completely invalidate the conventions and institutions found in a culture or subculture but modifies and redirects them. The conventions or institutions—whether political or medical institutions—are a valid source of knowledge about human nature, health and morals.

This is not to suggest that Anglicanism requires acceptance of the medical or legal status quo, for there is a proud tradition of Anglican social protest in America and elsewhere. Habits may be of habitual betrayal. But Anglicanism should not make such judgments without listening to and learning from the experience of those most closely involved. The theology begins with incarnation that leads to judgment; ethics begins with listening that leads to criticism.

The point was well made a few years ago by the Oxford philosopher of religion Basil Mitchell. He suggested that the social structure of a community could be compared "to an old and very rambling house which has grown over the centuries in a variety of styles, but which has nevertheless a distinct character of its own."[40] Mitchell goes on to note that such a house, even if very large, will have some features common to all houses and others that are peculiar to it in virtue of its history, location and owners. If remodeling is discussed, people living in the house can be expected to disagree about how much, or which portions, of the old structure to preserve.

The point I wish to make is that it is essential to Anglicanism to have some concern for and to be informed by the character, quality and identity of the one particular house, or society, where it finds itself. It can be quite Anglican to insist that the time has come for building a new west front, rebuilding the interior or tearing down a wing. But this tradition must always attend to the house—the institutions and conventions, religious and secular, of the community where it is. These conventions are both sources of insight and subjects of concern.

Anglicanism is a tradition of loyalty, nourished in worship, informed by the past, shaped by and committed to the culture from which it springs; it resists the idea that the only relevant social norms are laws passed by a civil government, for it insists that other institutions of society—notably the church—appropriately have a voice in shaping the social identity and habits of the community. Thus it is very characteristic of Anglicanism (and of this book) to be relatively sure about what practices vis à vis abortion or care for the dying should prevail—yet to be ambivalent about what role civil law should play in shaping society to that end. It is an ethic of community, conscience and compromise.

Nature

What I have said so far suggests that Anglican thought about human nature, ethics and health is naturalistic in a broad sense, for the metaphysical fact of the incarnation and cultural practices do serve as premises for moral judgments. They are facts, of a sort, from which value conclusions are inferred. To be sure they are value-saturated facts, but that may not change the structure of the logical problems presented. This context, however, is not the one in which to take up those philosophical issues.

Rather, it is important to note that Anglicanism has an ongoing tradition of looking not just to social tradition but to the natural world itself as a source of religious and moral knowledge. From Richard Hooker in the sixteenth century through Arthur Peacocke in this one, leading Anglican thinkers have wanted to reconcile religious and scientific knowledge, and the concept of natural law is always taken seriously, having been "rehabilitated" in this century by C. S. Lewis, Ian Ramsey and John Macquarrie, among others. On the one hand, Anglicans natively want to affirm the unity of truth; on the other hand, they are not content with cultural relativism and want to insist on a metaphysical grounding for at least a core of morality. They want a normative concept of the natural.

Theologically speaking this claim has both a negative and a positive side. Negatively it involves saying that the Bible and tradition are not sufficient bases for moral reasoning. Thus Hooker noticed that it is because we credit the judgment of others that we value scripture.[41] The Bible does teach us things necessary to salvation, but basic moral principles and duties are known apart from it. Scripture may be a sufficient source of information about salvation, but to infer that it is a sufficient basis for daily moral life puts individuals in an impossible bind and only serves to discredit the Bible's true authority.[42] Beyond scripture and tradition we require the guidance of nature.

More recently, J. F. D. Maurice's thought involved great stress on the incarnation, with some displacement of the moral teaching of Jesus. For Maurice, Jesus was "The Man," the divine humanity dreamed of by all ages and peoples. He was "a perfect being" who proved "his perfections by entering entirely into the lowest condition into which man has ever entered and actually rising into the highest of which man has ever dreamed."[43] But Jesus' teachings in the Sermon on the Mount (Matt. 5–7) should not be construed as a social code; he did not mean to prohibit the oath required of a witness in court, but to criticize defamation of all that is sacred, to rule out what we would call vulgarity as well as profanity. Retribution is to be *avoided* by *individuals*, whose conduct is to be regulated by the principle of endurance of private wrong, but retribution is *obligatory* for the *state* as "an image of the order and moral government of the world."[44] Gordon Dunstan, once Maurice Professor at King's College, London, notes that "the church of England, at the Reformation, formally renounced the doctrine that specific words of Jesus could be treated as legislative norms for a civil society." The last three of the Thirty-nine Articles "approve Christian participation in war, private ownership of property, and taking an oath before a magistrate. All of this runs contrary to the teaching of Jesus."[45] Maurice also thought Christian morals had to appeal to the nonrevealed or natural.

As this book proceeds it will be clear that I share this Anglican preoccupation, with the natural as norm, although I do not have a general theory of what is "natural" to present to the reader. Certainly I have been heavily influenced by the contemporary Jewish Aristotelian Leon Kass, and I think the influence of Aristotle (not only Aquinas) within Anglicanism is very great, but my method of work has not been to begin with a systematic discussion. Rather I have found an appeal to the natural to be the least problematic alternative in coping with some issues (see chapters 4 and 5) and I shall leave to another occasion—or other writers—the task of general theoretical construction.

Perhaps an illustration of why this issue comes up would be helpful. In *Morals and Medicine*, published in 1954, Joseph Fletcher offered the first major work in medical ethics in decades. His analysis of such issues as truthtelling, sterilization and euthanasia was based on a personalist account of human nature. "Physical nature," he wrote, "is what is over against us, out there. It represents the world of *its*. Only men and God are *thou*; they only are persons."[46] He continued: "It is the integrity of the personality that has first claim in the forum of conscience. To be a person . . . means to be free of physiology."[47] More positively, Fletcher argued that personhood involves freedom of choice and knowledge of options. Persons deprived of those things are victimized and degraded, reduced to the products of biology or social processes. From this starting point Fletcher was able to offer stinging criticisms of conservative theological moralists, especially of pre-Vatican II Catholics, but also of some Anglicans.[48] It has also led Fletcher to advocate sterilization of the retarded, active euthanasia, the energetic pursuit of eugenic goals and a libertarian view on abortion.

If these conclusions are problematical, it makes sense to wonder about Fletcher's premises, which pose a stark disjunction between self and body. Perhaps the premises are correct and the conclusions to be embraced, but at several points I will suggest that the conclusions are dubious enough to warrant a basic rethinking.

In any event, it should not be strange that concern with the natural is employed within Anglicanism. An established church is very likely to project its vision of the world onto a cosmic screen and call it "natural," although this tendency does not prove that perception of natural relations and processes is impossible. Furthermore, the incarnational core of Anglicanism virtually requires ascribing a kind of sacredness to the body, and if bodies are helpfully understood using transcultural categories (for example of nutrition) then some of the ingredients for the requisite theory about how nature is known are in place.

Enough of prologue. It is time to turn to some complexes of issues.

· 2 ·

Sharing

The central event in Anglican worship is the eucharist or holy communion. This regularly enacted ritual relates directly to the central events in Christian history, for it is a communal reenactment of the offering, death and resurrection of Christ. The core of it is an *anamnesis*, or recalling to mind, a process that is "the antithesis of amnesia. A person with amnesia has lost identity and purpose. To know who you are, to whom you belong, and where you are headed, you must remember."[1] In the eucharistic liturgy both the individual worshiper and the worshiping community are reminded of their identity.

This process is worked out macrocosmically in the eucharistic liturgy as a whole. Persons come to the place of worship; offer their money, food, drink and selves; see these blessed and broken; and are renewed by feeding on them again. The central movement of remembering, offering and blessing is formulated as follows in one version of the *Book of Common Prayer:*

> We celebrate the *memorial* of our redemption, O Father, in this sacrifice of praise and thanksgiving. *Recalling* his death, resurrection and ascension, we *offer* you these gifts.
>
> *Sanctify them* by your Holy Spirit to be for your people the Body and Blood of your Son, the holy food and drink of new and unending life in him. *Sanctify us* also that we may faithfully receive this holy Sacrament, and serve you in unity, constancy and peace; and at the last day bring us with all your saints into the joy of your eternal kingdom.[2]

The eucharist is a holy *communion*—between God and humankind and among persons.

This kind of communion can be interpreted in many different ways, but the important point for our purpose now is to note the effect on the persons who participate. These are twofold. They are exalted, and they are peculiarly involved with one another. Stress on these tendencies has sometimes been so strong as to be excessive within Anglicanism, but they remain important themes all the same. Charles Gore, the English bishop and scholar, wrote at the beginning of this century that "it is the humanity of nothing less than the divine person which is . . . communicated to us. . . ."[3] He continued:

> This—the propagation of Christ's manhood by the transmission of His Spirit, or Christ *in us* the hope of glory—is truly the culminating point of our religion, which alone explains the rest.[4]

Thus the liturgy suggests that participants are children of God—not slaves or servants. This at least reinforces, perhaps establishes, a general theme of the Anglican ethos. We stressed this theme in chapter 1 and will draw on it again.

The other effect of the eucharist is to make clear the sacredness of society, for within the ritual "the sacrifice is completed in communion."[5] The "body" that is offered, broken and renewed at the altar is, among other things, the social body of the community.[6] This idea derives from the Pauline writings, especially 1 and 2 Corinthians, and it can be carried to extremes as when Gore calls the church the "extension of the incarnation."[7] In fact the term "body of Christ" means different things at different points in Paul's letters, and it is clear—as Gore realized—that the symbolism is often more Christological than ecclesiological. But, at the least, Paul and the liturgical drama and symbols suggest that the community created in worship is an *image* of the Lord's life, a body of *adopted* children of the Father. The idea of the church as the body of Christ suggests the great importance of the religious community in particular and human community generally.

Although the liturgical drama forces those involved to think of themselves corporately, as a social body in which the bonds are sacred, the outer limits of this community are not clear. In the rehearsal of the acts of Christ remembered in the liturgy one version of the rite recalls, "He stretched out his arms upon the cross, and offered himself in obedience to your will, a perfect sacrifice for the whole world,"[8] a phrase which for the early fathers suggested the redemption of all peoples.[9] The community celebrated is not just the community present in the room but includes past and future worshipers and those "outside" the worshiping community as well. The church pervades and exists for the world.

Indeed, as I noted in chapter 1, Anglicans have trouble making clear boundaries for the church. Lambourne argued that communion with those who suffer is the true sacrament:

> There is a sense in which the mystical body is not the ecclesiastical apos-
> tolic congregation that we call the Church, but the mystical body of suf-
> fering men and women. Those who would join the mystical body must
> have communion with a sufferer. Not only in the consecrated elements,
> not only in the Church, but also in the sufferer does faith know the real
> presence and by communion with each partake of the spiritual Christ.[10]

To be in community with those who suffer is, in an important sense, to
be a part of the body of Christ.

The New Testament contains many metaphors to describe the church;
that of the "body of Christ" is theologically misleading if taken alone, for it
can suggest the perfection of the institutional church.[11] But the metaphor
does rightly call attention to the community-creating function of the
eucharistic liturgy in Anglicanism, to the fact that part of the salvation
dynamic is finding oneself brought into community with other persons, a
community that is therefore holy or sacred. It is this community that is the
subject of this chapter. Before taking up a set of specific problems, however, I want to note some general characteristics of community within
Anglicanism.

The first of these is that community is thought to involve interdependence. It is not strictly a matter of like-mindedness or ideological agreement, nor is it a revocable contract. Rather it involves a shared identity
and a notion that to live is to acknowledge one's dependencies, ultimately
upon God. Ethically, as we have seen, the logical expression of this fact is a
demand of fidelity. The importance of this emphasis within Anglicanism
comes out in theologies of marriage, which tend to stress the creation of an
ontological bond that persons can neither decide to break nor wish into
nonexistence (although it may, in fact, die). The worship of the church
suggests that whether we like it or not we live in and for each other and
that estrangement will finally prove to be limited. Jeremy Taylor put the
point very well:

> God gave necessities to men, that all might need: and several abilities to
> several persons, that each man might help to supply the public needs, and
> by joining to fill up all wants, they may be knit together by justice, as the
> parts of the world are by nature.[12]

Our need for one another is not a liability but is thought to be providential.

Secondly, interdependent life has some stability. Relationships take on a
form, persons are cast in specific roles. Community is not abstract but has
a kind of structure. This is clear in the polity of the church, which

Anglicans take with great seriousness. There is a definite role for bishops, priests, deacons and laity—parameters that define the extraordinarily diverse ways in which incumbents may play their roles. Furthermore, expectations may be associated with other roles—of political leader, for example. Exactly what is expected of the incumbent bishop, king, president or deacon has changed and will continue to change, but it is characteristic of Anglicanism to think that acceptance of community, consent to social being, involves a willingness to live in a situation in which one does not claim to make every decision for oneself but allows a social division of labor.

This said, there is a complex dialectic within Anglicanism on the issue of centralized power versus individual choice. On the one hand the communion insists on a symbolic unification of power in the episcopate. This requirement is not just a matter of formal polity and liturgical order, but shows up sometimes in not very attractive attitudes toward bishops—excessive deference in their presence, backbiting in their absence—on the part of priests and deacons. Even in the American church, bishops have significant power, as do clergy within congregations. Certain matters, characteristically involving worship and the ordination of clergy, are within the special provenance of priest or bishop.

Among other things this arrangement implies the community's willingness to acknowledge expertise. In another era, Hooker argued that with respect to issues "obscure, intricate and hard to be judged of" those who had invested a lifetime of study in the issue rightly appear as guides for their less well-informed neighbors.[13] Authority within the community is not, in principle, dubious.

On the other hand, the power of ecclesiastics is always checked: by each other, by crown or Parliament or, at least in the case of the American church, by the laity. The clergy do not control the money in parish or diocese, and they are chosen by representatives of those units rather than being sent in from outside. They do not set their own salaries, which are controlled by the laity. One liturgical symbol of this relationship in contemporary American worship is the passing of the peace, a process that is initiated by the celebrant, but does *not* pass down from him but rather bubbles up within the congregation.[14] The priest is a leader of the people and for the people of God, which is why after confessing with them he can turn and in God's name pronounce absolution on them.[15]

Thus the community of worship is one of interdependence, with stable roles in which power is shared and responsibilities devolve upon specific persons. No one is good enough to be trusted with unchecked power; indeed, empowerment is so important that it must extend throughout the community. But this distribution of power is not fundamentally equalitarian in the sense that everyone's role is the same. For role differentiation is assumed to be essential to community; community cannot exist if persons are unwilling to give up some responsibility for themselves. The crucial idea is exchange or caring for another.

If community is looked at this way, some issues in medicine appear in a new light. I wish to take up three general topics to illustrate this point: sharing power, sharing knowledge and sharing resources.

SHARING POWER

One of the hardest questions in modern medicine is who should make difficult decisions, especially about the termination of life support, but in other areas as well ranging from resource allocation to genetic engineering. One crisp position on this issue might roughly be described as "all power to the professional," the suggestion being that decisions are rightly made by physicians, economists or geneticists. So simply stated, this viewpoint in which sovereignty is located solely in the expert is rightly unpopular today, and it fits poorly with the Anglican notion of community that I have tried to describe. At the other extreme, and arising as a protest against the first model, is a powerfully articulated and defended view of patients' rights. Broadly speaking the philosophical viewpoint underlying this stance is Kantian: Persons as autonomous subjects should be masters of their own fate. The idea is well captured in the title of the play, *Whose Life Is It, Anyway?*

Strong strands of Anglican tradition support this view, articulated with great force by Joseph Fletcher in *Morals and Medicine*. Human dignity involves thinking and deciding for oneself, he contends, and the church should forthrightly stand for human dignity. Therefore persons should have a right to decide for their own death and require the truth; they should have unfettered control over their reproductive lives.

Profound as these claims are, they are not ultimately adequate from an Anglican perspective, because they are too individualistic: The basic model seems to be that of the sovereign self, which can interpret actions upon it only as threats to its mastering of its world. This notion is the very idea that the holy communion rejects. In it, communicants surrender their sick selves and receive back a renewed and refreshed being. True selfhood is found in the social, communal interaction of the ritual, not in isolation.

The whole idea of holy communion is that power is shared; it is not rightly the possession of one person, even if that person should choose to give it away. For giving can alienate giver and recipient. Michael Wilson has made this point by telling a story of Martin of Tours who, on Wilson's account, chose to share his cloak against the elements with someone, rather than simply giving it to him, although giving may at first seem the higher moral value. But by *sharing* Martin established community, and it is sharing that is at the heart of the eucharist.[16]

From this perspective the issue of medical power is misconceived if we say, "Doctors now have the power, and they should give it to patients," for this imperative perpetuates an alienating model in which the idea of sharing continues to be excluded. Of course it is true that patients, as adopted children of the Father, should more often have final voice than they now have. But the reason for this adjustment is their unique familiarity with themselves and others affected; it is, so to speak, a special role they are called on to play within the community, and only as such a matter of individual right. This is a general point for now, but I shall begin to fill it out in subsequent chapters.

Are individual and health professionals the only appropriate parties to medical decision-making? What should be the relationship between organized religion and medical decision-making? Michael Wilson rightly sees that this question raises a fundamental issue of the relationship between religious and medical institutions. Churches sometimes have seen hospitals as an aid to be *given* to the poor, but this view can be condescending. Equally unsatisfactory are images of the hospital as mission field or covert arm of the church. Rather, Wilson argues, the church should support the work of hospitals, but as responsible children of God, i.e., encouraged to make critical judgments. The church and her staff in hospitals have a special role in dealing with the sick, and it is the pursuit of truth:

> The primary task of the church is in . . . the search for truth, the handing on of truth, the reinterpretation and renewal of truth, and the communication of truth, for its bearing upon what it means to be human in a situation of wellness or illness and for the health of society.[17]

This general viewpoint has strong implications for the role of the religious professional in a hospital setting, for it suggests that such a person, a chaplain for instance, should not see himself or herself primarily in terms of the therapeutic expectations of the hospital. Chaplains should not, Wilson rightly says, exchange the Christian model of health in community for a medical model of "wellness through the eradication of defects."[18] The distinctive identity of the religious professional suggests she cannot be seen simply as a member of the therapeutic team, because her identity includes Jesus' identification with the sick, not with the healer (e.g., Matt. 25), and a recognition of the fact that not all suffering is an appropriate target for medical cure.[19]

John Fletcher reinforces this point. The clergy counselor, he says, should not too quickly become anyone's advocate. In dealing with individuals or a family in crisis, the first pastoral move is to be honest with one's self and to take the lead in expressing shock, pain or anger.[20] The time may come when the identity and tradition of the community of faith are appropriately unfolded, but the fundamental responsibility is honestly to be present, identified with the suffering, and honestly reacting to the pain.

In addition to standing for truth about self and fate while in the hospital, religious professionals should make sure that the recognition of sickness and illness can become a reality in congregational worship, so that worship can serve as a communion of the sick and a strengthening resource for persons in anticipation of their future role as patients. Lambourne's sentence—"the sickness situation must itself be made an offertory"[21]—is an excellent one. He suggests that those who are ill bring the bread and wine to the altar for consecration; health professionals, in contrast, might bring "that cup of cold water which symbolizes the Real Presence of Christ at deeds of mercy." And then these persons should receive communion together so "the local congregation may see their sickness–healing situation made by the work of Christ their salvation situation." The same kind of process can go on in homes where a family, not just the person who is ill, receives the sacrament. [N]othing could be nearer to the heart of the New Testament than a vital group of people taking Communion about their representative on the sick bed."[22] The church should insist on a sharing of power and itself should share both by human presence and by enabling community among the sick and the healthy, healed and healer.

SHARING KNOWLEDGE

For power to be shared, so must knowledge be. But this has not always been the case in medicine and the issues are complicated.

Historically Anglicanism has insisted on the importance of truth. In *Morals and Medicine* Joseph Fletcher offered a strong defense of the responsibility of telling patients the truth. He reasoned that persons have a right to make decisions for themselves, which they cannot do without knowledge. Therefore physicians have an obligation to tell the truth, even if the patient does not ask for it, although Fletcher concedes that a patient's expressed wish not to know should be respected.[23] The general framework he presupposes is built around the dignity of the autonomous individual, and the abuse that he wants to avoid is that of benevolent deception, keeping information from the patient allegedly to spare the patient misery and preserve hope, but really to avoid inconvenience and embarrassment for the health professional.

Trenchant as this observation is, it skates around two kinds of problems. One of them is the complexity of human communication about serious matters affecting the communicators themselves, for it is a commonplace that we often fail to hear what others say or ask. Perspectives on ourselves and problems of self-deception are so complicated that a general responsibility to tell the truth, while important, remains abstracted from the kinds of questioning and answering that go on in medical encounters.

Second, for this reason, Fletcher's rights-centered approach can lead to the unfortunate suggestion that accuracy is a *sufficient* criterion for moral speech: So long as I told the truth, I did the right thing. The trouble with this position is that the truth can be used to intimidate or terrify someone; it can be formulated in words unintelligible to the patient, or it can be spoken in a verbal or social context that converts it to a form of desertion.

I think it better to insist that the fundamental responsibility to sick persons is fidelity, being true to them. This bond of trust is eroded by lying "and trust is too precious, too essential, in professional relationships to be so put in jeopardy."[24] In the 1920s Kenneth Kirk, the bishop and Oxford moralist, made this same kind of point. Kirk worried that an overly rigorous insistence on a principle like "Never lie" would lead to a casuistical process that was disingenuous and only served to discredit moral reasoning. He rejected the idea of differentiating among lies strictly on the basis of motive. The core of his argument is the idea that truth is demanded as a component of relationships of trust, loyalty and confidence—either between individuals or between individuals and groups. A lie is wrong insofar as it betrays the trustworthy character of individual or group. One of his illustrations concerns a seriously ill woman whose son has died. She asks about his fate. If she asks a *doctor*, Kirk will *allow a lie* for

> a reasonable patient would recognize that it is a doctor's business to save life whenever possible. She might be grieved that he thought her too frail to hear the truth; but her outlook on life would not be seriously altered, nor would the reputation either of the particular doctor or of the medical profession suffer.

In contrast, Kirk thinks a *priest could not lie* for:

A priest's business is with the soul rather than with the body, and among the spiritual results which he is specially bound to consider and promote is exactly that respect for veracity which we regard as essential to human intercourse. His lie would not merely suggest that he—although peculiarly commissioned to safe-guard the credit of truthfulness—was careless to its claims; it might also lower the dignity of truthfulness itself in the estimation of the sufferer. . . .

Along similar lines, Kirk argues the woman's *husband* must *answer truthfully* because of their familial relationship.[25]

Kirk did not see that his argument about distrust could apply to the *medical profession* as well as to the clergy, but he did see, rightly, that the requirements of honest speech modulate with the forms of relationships or loyalty.[26] Physicians do have a responsibility honestly to answer questions they may be asked, but this requirement is only part of the requirement of medical truth. To see what else might be involved we will take one contemporary application.

In *Coping with Genetic Disorders* John C. Fletcher defends an assertive theory of truthful communication. Clergy are to be "faithful companions" at times when religious need is great, namely at times of stress and crisis. Religion is "a process for making sense in ourselves when conflicts that arise from the condition of being human threaten to tear apart our basic confidence that we are worthwhile." When persons face crises of meaning and assurance, the role of the faithful companion is to provide "help to face the full meaning and impact of every terror, especially death." The companion helps me to "learn the meaning of life without resort to illusion or injustice."[27]

Thus within counseling it is especially important to seek truth. This begins in acknowledgment of one's own feelings. After they are in touch with themselves, counselors should help clients to do the same thing. The client will dodge by failing to speak in the first-person singular. Since "to sin" means "to miss the point or evade . . . evasion that results in self-deception is Public Enemy Number One in being a faithful companion in moral deliberations." In pushing for the truth clergy test themselves and others, protect themselves against trouble later, and enable a process of religious growth.[28]

Thus, on Fletcher's terms, the objective of verbal (and presumably non-verbal) companionship is relentless pursuit of the truth. In premarital counseling, for example, the religious processes involved are those of "separation and new beginnings." If Fletcher receives from a *parent* a request to celebrate the marriage of her child, he may respond "I'm interested to

hear about it, but I really prefer to be contacted by the couple themselves."
Or "Did they ask you to call me?" Or "Why are *you* calling me?"

> The immediate reaction of the parent may be bristling irritation, but you
> [the clergyperson] can decide not to let the temporary security of being
> popular with the parent interfere with the job of being a good companion
> to both couple and parents. If more is needed by the parents to remind
> them that they are off-target, simply ask if they plan to be doing things
> like this for the rest of their lives.[29]

His operative principle is that family relationships "thrive on direct communication of thoughts and feelings and tend to become troubled and even
pathological if communication is indirect or through third parties."[30]

The cases Fletcher reports from his own practice show him practicing
what he preaches. No one who is in touch with Fletcher should expect him
to be a background member of the cast. His pursuit of honesty can involve
power. His involvement is conditional on others meeting his requirements,
and he expects them to engage in realpolitik. For example, he was asked to
celebrate the marriage of an older couple. The woman's grown daughter
had objections, and she refused to meet to talk things over. Fletcher then
asked his client two questions:

> "Do you have anything in your will about leaving her something?" She
> answered yes. "Have you learned anything in your career as a successful
> stockbroker that would help you with your daughter? You have clout
> with her, but you are not using it." I told Jeanne that without the meeting,
> I could not take a chance on going ahead. Within an hour, I had a tele-
> phone call from Jeanne's daughter, saying that the meeting would be at
> her home.[31]

Fletcher realizes that this brisk approach may alienate some people. He
dislikes that, but

> I comfort myself by asking if I want to risk my own integrity and self-
> respect by standing at the altar with a couple about whom statements are
> made as to their adequacy as adults when they have, in fact, evaded their
> responsibility. I do not enjoy being disliked, but I do enjoy some new-
> found self-respect in my conduct as a minister.[32]

My reaction to this theory is ambivalent. Fletcher rightly sees that the
quest for truth leads beyond verbal veracity to truthful relationship. His
vigorous pursuit of that goal, leading him to cut through self-deception

and pretense, is refreshing. Obviously a concern for integrity is something of great importance. But something has gone wrong.

Our initial negative reaction may be to say that Fletcher is being a bit manipulative with the authority of his office. He insists on setting the terms for encounters. Although he does not impose ideas or even much in the way of behavioral restriction, he maintains power (which comes from other persons) and does not risk powerlessness. In particular he uses verbal power. In fact, there is some ambiguity in his thought on the role of words. I have tried to show that they are important as a direct access to the issue in marriage counseling. But when dealing with parents of a malformed newborn, Fletcher says that "above all" faithful companions (clergy) "need not talk *about* the religious process. The proper concern should be to recognize what is going on, leading and participating at the same time." In this way they "model" participation in the religious process.[33] But Fletcher seems to have "talked about" the religious process with his clients already referred to (to say nothing of others in the book), and it must be obvious that a claim to "recognize what is going on" is an awesome claim. What makes the faithful companion's perception special?

Fletcher's mistake is to think persons can always decide whether or not to be in a relationship of faithful companionship. Thus he thinks of truth as a precondition for the relationship. But there are many contexts, perhaps including genetic counseling and celebration of marriage, where being in relationship is nonnegotiable. The first business in such a situation is establishment of a relationship of trust. This goal is not necessarily achieved by enunciation of the true (i.e., the faithful companion's) agenda (or facts) at the outset, for that may not be the time when truth can be heard. As Fletcher somewhere observes, the *first* preparation for faithful companionship in crisis is establishing a history or pattern of companioning. Once that pattern is established, then truth may be pushed, as Fletcher wants to do. He doesn't take seriously enough the issue of *when* to speak the truth. He is right to insist on speaking it; he is wrong to insist on it as the first chord.

Furthermore, it is not at all clear that the truth of relationships can be perceived or verbalized as clearly as Fletcher may assume. His indictment of indirection cuts through us all, but a sacramental religion is committed to mediation, and the metaphors that inform tradition instruct us without being unequivocally true. If our worship and talk of God reflect this humility, should we not expect to find parallel subtleties in talk about matters of ultimate human importance? Faithful companionship requires learning to listen and talk to others in more than one key.

Thus, as Cicely Saunders once wrote, the real issue is not so much *telling* as it is *listening* and responding. Preoccupation with telling the truth perpetuates the idea of a professional who is in charge. "The real question is not 'what do you tell your patients?' but rather 'what do you let your patients tell you?' Learn to hear what they are saying; what they are not saying; what is hidden underneath; what *is* going on."[34] Therefore:

> The rule is that there are no general rules here except that you must listen. You must be ready to listen; you must be ready to be silent; and you must just be committed . . . it should be hard to tell. You . . . should not be doing this easily. It *should* be hard because you are trying to bring everything you have of understanding to hear what this patient is really asking you.[35]

For individuals to be empowered, information must be shared. But responsibilities for that sharing are diverse. As Kirk suggests, it may sometimes be best if bad news comes from someone other than the doctor, and our fundamental concern with truth derives from a web of fidelity and trust. Michael Wilson put it well:

> Communication in hospital is not simply a matter of ensuring that information passes from one person to another. This is not unimportant. But in the human encounters of a hospital ward we communicate more than information—we share our fears and joys, love and hate; *in fact we communicate ourselves to one another.* We listen not just to words but to one another. Truth, in fact, is personal. The admission of this and the cost it involves in human terms, is an essential part of what it means to be a doctor, a nurse or a patient. But the hospital gets the lesson wrong: it focuses attention upon the communication of information, and the fully informed patient may yet starve for lack of communion with his fellow human beings.[36]

To which I add only: Not only hospitals, but moralists (religious and not) also "get the lesson wrong." Truth must be told in and by fidelity.

SHARING RESOURCES

In addition to knowledge and power, eucharistic life involves some suggestions about the distribution or allocation of the human, capital and technical resources involved in health care. In *Spheres of Justice*, Michael Walzer offers some suggestions that Anglicans should find striking.

Walzer's general thesis is that *justice* is misunderstood if considered primarily as a matter of individual rights. Instead he insists that the fundamental social category is *membership* in a community. Selves are the products of communities that have a particular history and identity. Thus communities differ from one another and change over time.

One thing communities always do, to some degree, is meet need. To be sure they do not agree about what it is that members of the community need: It may be freedom, or defense, or bread or aspirin. But once a community begins to provide needed goods, it should distribute them in accordance with need. In the abstract there is little or nothing that any society must recognize as a need, but once society has recognized a need, then the need itself provides criteria for its distribution. Meeting recognized needs is not a matter of surplus. "Socially recognized needs are the first charge against the social product."[37]

Walzer notes that in the Middle Ages the human need for salvation was widely recognized. In cathedral and parish church, by monks and secular clergy, society attempted to meet religious needs. Today we are more this-worldly; the need for a secure afterlife is not acknowledged by the secular state, which looks to the present instead. Health has replaced heaven as our preoccupation. We acknowledge the need of persons for health. But, Walzer argues, no comparable shift in institutions has occurred, for we do not in fact deliver needed health care to all.

> So long as communal funds are spent, as they currently are, to finance research, build hospitals and pay the fees of doctors in private practice, the services that these expenditures underwrite must be equally available to all citizens.[38]

The suggestion is that within their own frame of reference our medieval forefathers did a better job of communal provision than we do, for they acknowledged in principle a social duty to meet the most fundamental need of everyone.

Then, as now, these needs cannot be met without cost, and one cost, central to the American tradition, will be liberty—notably, in this case, the market liberty of physicians. Just as the medieval church could not begin to deliver on its social responsibilities if clergy were completely free to function as unchecked entrepreneurs, so some kinds of constraints will be necessary to assure that less-attractive specialties, populations and geographical areas receive adequate medical care. For the sake of need, some trade-offs against liberty are justified.

Note, however, that these are not necessarily trade-offs against the physician's clinical freedom or authority, discussed earlier in this chapter and elsewhere. Nor do I think that the argument for social provision of medical care necessarily requires the formation of a national health service, for society and the state are distinguishable entities. It may be that tax and educational incentives, philanthropy (including that of the churches) and emerging patterns of organization of health-care delivery can discharge our social obligation adequately—perhaps better than a national health service could do. However, even though Aaron and Schwartz may be right when they judge that "the United States is not interested in creating a national health service on the British model,"[39] the communion-centered nature of the Anglican ethic is such as to require consideration of public responsibility for providing medical care.

Even here there are ambiguities. Not all "medical" needs are created equal. Acknowledging a need for chemotherapy should not force us to argue that orthodontia, all cosmetic surgery and heart transplants are equally needed. We have to make some judgments about the relative importance of some of these needs. The general thrust of this book suggests the importance of primary care[40] and hospice or comparable services at the end of life, and a lower priority that might be assigned to infertility treatments of all kinds. Thus some form of rationing, the "painful prescription" to which Aaron and Schwartz refer, is not only inevitable but appropriate for a community whose medical goal is a healthy life in which finitude is acknowledged.

Finally, however, it must be clear that no Anglican vision can require a particular set of priorities within health care. What it can demand is an acknowledgment of the public obligation. The church in its preaching and teaching can nurture an ideal of life in which morality is accepted in hope and joy; it can be a community where service is offered in worship and at the bedside; and it can invest its monetary and human resources in the provision of care. I will try to spell out part of what that involves in the rest of this book.

· 3 ·

Mortality

MYSELF

Dying is not what it was. There was a time when people could assume that they would die relatively young, quickly and at home. In the Western world those days are gone forever. The causes of death have changed. Our grandparents and great-grandparents could expect to die of infectious diseases or accidents. We, on the other hand, know that we are most likely to die of cardiovascular problems or of malignancies. That means that most of us will have longer lives than our grandparents, and that these longer lives will end in a rather lengthy period of physical and mental decline. We can expect that our last days will not be spent surrounded by our families but in institutions miles away from our homes.

We must recognize, in other words, that the wonderful developments in modern medicine that have prolonged and in many ways improved our lives have had the result of making our *dying* worse. Death, we might say, is no news flash. It is something people have always thought about. What is changed in the modern era is the circumstances of dying, and it is quite plausible to say that some of the medical developments that have been associated with improvement of our health have also been associated with vexing our dying.

How shall we think about death and dying in this new context, one in which "because cure is so highly valued, death is the great technological failure."[1]

The starting point for this reasoning must be the basic conviction of the goodness of life as part of the fundamental goodness of the created world. A world in which God participates and which he created is a world confessed to be good. Consequently there is always something lost in death, something to be mourned. As the end of something good, and as separation, death is a bad thing.

Thus fear and dread of death are natural and appropriate. Death is not a subject that can be completely sanitized. Elisabeth Kübler-Ross and others have helpfully stressed the value of acceptance of death, but no acceptance of death is easy and there are limits beyond which an acceptance of death should not go. The Anglican theologian Jeremy Taylor wrote three hundred years ago that there is nothing wrong with groaning, shrieking or losing one's composure when ill or near death. The fear of death is something we may be lucky enough to avoid, he continued, but even the boldest experience it. "Our Blessed Lord was pleased to legitimate fear to us, by his agony and prayers in the garden. It is not a sin to be afraid, but it is a great felicity to be without fear."[2]

We can plausibly say, however, that death is a good thing in at least two senses. The first arises if we presume to take God's point of view on the world. Should God have designed a world in which people die? Probably, because death makes change possible. The fact that one generation succeeds another builds flexibility and adaptibility into the human species. If no one ever died, the world would be a stodgy, boring kind of place, and there would be fewer possibilities that human beings might realize. Of course death can be untimely, but note that a changing of the guard, a shift from one generation to another, is probably a very good thing in the world.

Taylor's speculations on this matter are instructive. In the Garden of Eden, he contends, earthly life could not have gone on indefinitely, for problems of overcrowding would inevitably have resulted. Thus, even if Adam had not sinned, God would have moved him out of the world. The punitive character of death that the Fall story portrays is neither the separation of soul and body nor departure from historical existence. Those changes or departures are part of the good created order. Ideal man is not immortal. What is a curse is "the manner of going," i.e., by "a natural diminution and aptness to disease and misery." Before the Fall life was "a happy duration"; subsequently it has become "a daily and miserable change."[3] Death in itself and as such is not so bad; sickness, decay and discomfort are the evils.

In addition, Taylor is suggesting a relationship between the core human problem of sin, symbolized in the Fall, and the discomforts associated with sickness and death. Because death is inevitable, a part of even the ideal world, true improvement in life must come from leading a virtuous life. Our lives are long enough for virtue, if not for worldly ambition. A life of self-recollection and prayer and fasting need not seem short. What we need to do to make our lives good does not take much time.

The core of Taylor's view is the idea that a person is a "bubble," "mushroom" or "vapor"—a transitory and perishable creature. Perhaps unconsciously, we are inevitably aware of our mortality. Changes we observe such as aging, loss of baby teeth, the blossoming and wilting of flowers are prefigurations of death. Death is inevitable for all—rich and poor—and it may come at any time. Therefore we should make the best use of the present, for "this instant will never return again, and yet it may be this instant will declare or secure the fortune of a whole eternity."[4]

Taylor is referring in part to rewards and punishments in a next life, but more than that he is pointing out that the fact of death leads to some good results in this world. Contemplation of my own mortality and the mortality of those I love has excellent effects on me. It makes me take my life seriously.

We all live with deadlines. An article has to be done by the first of the month. "The paper is due a week from Thursday." "Your test is going to be given May fourteenth, and that's the only day it is going to be given." These deadlines are a way of establishing the fact that there is a certain limited time frame within which a particular job must be done, and they make us get the job done. Moreover, not only do I have deadlines for myself, but others have deadlines as well. Each moment in their lives is unique and matters and is not to be shrugged off. I will live with my children in my home only for so many years. They will be high-school sophomores or high-school seniors only once, and those are moments that I have to capitalize on as best I can as they occur.

To the best of our knowledge, death marks a terminus beyond which I won't be able to do anything *for*, or *with*, or *to* anybody else, and the fact that those I love experience a similar deadline doubles the ante. Death forces me to realize that I have limited time to perform acts of love or acts of kindness and to rectify injustice; because it makes me take myself and others seriously, it is a tremendous source of drive and energy and a stimulus to human accomplishment. If I had indefinite time I could always procrastinate.

Thus Taylor argued that his book *Holy Dying* is not intended for the dying. Rather it is addressed to those alive and well, so that they may be prepared to die well. Taylor disagreed with the Catholicism of his day, which seemed to him to be concerned simply with confession and unction at the end of life. He could have said, with many a twentieth-century writer, that their mistake was failing to see that death is a part of life.[5]

Awareness of death and sickness cures our preoccupation with triviality. "One fit of the stone [he means the pain of kidney stones] takes away from the fancies of men all relations to the world and secular interests: at least they are made dull and flat, without sharpness and an edge."[6] Sickness and death can put things in perspective and serve to concentrate the mind.

This seeming celebration of sickness and death is troubling to the modern mind. It strikes us as morbid. But is it morbid to cut through pretense and to think seriously about fate? Doing so, Taylor thought, would lead us to avoid a "soft, delicate and voluptuous life" in favor of one that is "severe and holy." By thinking about death, he suggested, we are pushed to self-examination. As we come to know ourselves we will repent betrayals and harms we have done and be pushed away from lives caught up in "the labyrinths of care and impertinent affairs" and toward "a quiet and dis-entangled life."[7]

There is a sense, then, in which we need to learn to despise the world if we are to have any seriousness as persons. Without this we can have no courage, and "death hastens to a fearful man."[8] One role of the church is to help people in achieving this perspective. Hooker claimed that ritual fast-ing furthers this process for it can help persons separate better from worse desires. Arguably fasts are more fundamental than public festivals, since "grief is of necessity a more familiar guest" than joy.[9]

This negative chord in our thought about death should, finally, be set in a more positive context. Sickness, Taylor writes, is not a good without the grace of God. Trying to comfort someone with no sense of God's presence can lead only to fatalism; such a patient can learn only "the degree of his ca-lamity." But if sickness is seen as "a messenger from a chastising Father,"[10] we can put it to good use. It is true that our religion, as Taylor writes, finds salvation not in the avoidance of suffering but only after a willingness to embrace it, but the gospel, as Michael Wilson claims, offers *life* through death. This is the pattern of Jesus' life, confessed by Christians to be the basic form of reality. "God is a life-through-death God."[11] This process of dying and coming to new life is regularly reenacted throughout worship, but the crucial liturgical context for it is baptism.

Baptism is rightly presented as a celebration of new birth, but the theme of death must precede that of birth in the rite. The baptized individual first *dies* with Christ and then rises with him. It is tragic that this connection be-tween the dying we all must face and the death symbolized in baptism has largely been lost in the contemporary church, for baptism needs to involve a reminder of human infirmity and mortality. Once that context is estab-lished baptism is

> the first great sacrament of healing. By his baptism the sick man is already a member of the regenerated creation and the healing church. . . . He is joined to a therapeutic community in which the members both heal and receive healing. He is admitted as a healer and as one in need of being healed.[12]

Consistent with this conjunction of realism and hope, the American prayer book in its thanksgiving over the water of baptism includes the words: "We thank you, Father, for the water of Baptism. In it we are buried with Christ in his death. By it we share in his resurrection. Through it we are reborn by the Holy Spirit."[13] But it is rare for a sermon or homily to focus on the second of those sentences.

The initiation rite of baptism is a public acknowledgment of the inevitability of death and suffering for human beings. It involves an acceptance of this fate and a dedication of both the baptized and the congregation to a renewed life identified with Christ as children of God. Life for the Christian is always the life of someone who has already died. This perspective on life is vapid nonsense if it does not mean increased sensitivity to the suffering and death to be found in the world. This is not easy, for "in practice sensitiveness hurts. . . . We soon find that any increase in our sensitiveness to what is lovely in the world increases also our capacity for being hurt."[14]

One of the reasons it is important for baptism to be a part of the regular public worship of a congregation is that a consciousness of having died from loneliness to hope and membership in a saving community is not easy to maintain. People need to be reminded of who they are and what they live for, which is to love and care, not to stay around forever. Medical technology is truly wonderful, but it is "no substitute for the discovery of something to which to give your life which is more important than just prolonging it."[15] Suffering should be relieved, and technology is a great aid to this end. A long life is rightly the occasion for celebration. But a consciousness of community with God and others, which is the Christian hope, is in fact impossible without acknowledgment of the truth that involved selves suffer.

This realism and acceptance of limit may mean that there are cures available that people rightly reject. Michael Wilson cites the example of a blind healer who rejects his friends' prayers for recovery of his sight. The issue had been decided for him already:

> For in his blindness God gave him an exceptional gift of intuition into the hearts of those whom he could hear but could not see. He was afraid of losing this gift.[16]

People often have a duty to get well, and passive fatalism is rightly unpopular, but it seems hard to prejudge what acceptance of the finitude of life may involve. As Wilson says, we rightly find ourselves dealing with "voluntary activity and involuntary submission . . . we do well not to dogmatize, but humbly to meet each sufferer in his or her need, sitting where they sit, and helping them towards a knowledge of God's love for them."

OTHERS

Anglican thinking about death, we have said, culminates in the conviction that death and suffering are endurable because of the community created by God with persons and among them. This thought naturally leads to the question of forms of ministry to those who are immediately confronting sickness and death. Of course one such form is medical, and we shall speak more of that below. But other dimensions of this care should be mentioned.

The first of these involves establishing community with the sick. Liturgically this process is referred to as the visitation of the sick, the laying on of hands, or unction. It is important that the procedures not be seen simply as carrying some sort of magical potion, whether it be special oils or a reserved sacrament, to someone who is ill. The actions, whether of touching, anointing, feeding or talking are not just actions done by the healthy to the diseased. Rather, the

> participant observers identify themselves with the . . . sickness and sin visibly symbolized in the sick man. They offer themselves, together with the sick man's offering of himself, to Christ and God anoints them and him with his Spirit, giving them power to be little Christs in this sickness situation.[17]

Visitation of the sick is a social event, even if the society involved is only a very small group—perhaps made up only of patient, priest and family. The ritual procedures minister not only to the sick but to those we normally think of as care givers, who are acknowledged to be themselves in need of care. "The innocent suffering situation" Lambourne continues, "becomes in unction a remembrance of Christ's unmerited suffering by which men and women enter into a new life."

Consistent with this idea, the service for "Ministration to the Sick" in the American prayer book has three parts—a ministry of the word, a laying on of hands and anointing, and a communion. Any or all may be used. Unfortunately the anointing and laying on of hands section does not make the neediness of the priest and family as clear as it might, but the prayers stress spiritual courage, renewal and comfort at least as much as hope for medical cure. Choice of prayers is provided to adjust to what can honestly be expected in the situation. The permanently infirm need not be exhorted to "go out into the world." There are excellent prayers for wholeness of body and soul, health professionals, and for use before an operation. Consider

> Sanctify, O Lord, the sickness of your servant N., that the sense of his/her weakness may add strength to his/her faith and seriousness to his/her repentance; and grant that he/she may live with you in everlasting life; through Jesus Christ our Lord.
>
> O God, the source of all health: So fill my heart with faith in your love, that with calm expectancy I may make room for your power to possess me, and gracefully accept your healing; through Jesus Christ our Lord.
>
> Lord Jesus Christ, by your patience in suffering you hallowed earthly pain and gave us the example of obedience to your Father's will: Be near me in my time of weakness and pain; sustain me by your grace, that my strength and courage may not fail; heal me according to your will; and help me always to believe that what happens to me here is of little account if you hold me in eternal life, my Lord and my God.
>
> This is another day, O Lord. I know not what it will bring forth, but make me ready, Lord, for whatever it may be. If I am to stand up, help me to stand bravely. If I am to sit still, help me to sit quietly. If I am to lie low, help me to do it patiently. And if I am to do nothing, let me do it gallantly. Make these words more than words, and give me the Spirit of Jesus.

These (or other) prayers, together with a communion celebration, serve to establish a general tone of honesty in the face of illness as well as community or solidarity in affliction.

This honest community, however, has another important dimension. Obviously sickness should not be thought of as punitive, but, as Lambourne put it, it is "invariably an occasion on which . . . possible aetiological factors are to be borne in mind."[18] That is, when they are ill, people engage in spiritual self-examination.

One role of the church is to assist in this process. Many abuses are possible. The objective is not some kind of once-for-all deathbed inquisition or repentance, but inspection of the whole course of life. Back in the seventeenth century, Taylor thought a visit that was to involve self-examination should be done when the patient "can be conversed with and instructed. . . . When he understands or can be taught to understand, the case of the soul, and the rules of his conscience." That is, the minister was to be summoned *before* a last crisis. And the issues to be discussed may take more than one sitting. "To dress a soul for funeral is not a work to be dispatched at one meeting."[19]

In the course of these visits, Taylor thought, the clergy were not to be completely passive. Their first duty is exhorting the sick man to confess. Most people will want to get along with a vague "general and indefinite" confession; some habitual sinners will not realize they have any problem at all; all will gloss over omissions. Thus the priest must "awaken the lethargy and prick the conscience," stressing the fires of hell and the goal of avoiding them through the gospel.

The priest's objective was to be of help. It is in the patient's interest for his conscience to be clear. Normally a sick person gets the point, but "if he will not understand when he is secretly prompted, he must be hallooed to, and asked in plain interrogatives concerning the crime of his life." Taylor wrote *Holy Dying* for a rich patron. He adds that this radical spiritual therapy is to be pursued "without partiality, fear or interest" because it is no favor to a prince "to let him perish for the want of an honest, just and a free homily." The priest is not to be snoopy and inquisitive, but he is looking for a confession that is "particular and enumerative of the variety of evils which have disordered his life."

What if this confession is not forthcoming? Taylor believed in the legitimacy of excommunication as the church's acknowledgment of God's judgment on serious public sins. But he would *not* deny the communion on the sickbed. It is "no part of a divine commandment that any man should be denied to receive the communion if he desires it, and if he be in any probable capacity of receiving it." The minister should celebrate the sacrament if asked, so long as a form of repentance has been followed. Profession of repentance is enough, for the minister can judge only outward acts. Of course, the sick person must be warned of the dangers of a duplicitous or inadequate confession. Notoriously wicked persons are neither to be invited to nor refused the sacrament; they must simply be warned of the risks of all courses of action.[20]

The notion of "hallooing to" a notorious sinner is one that is rather out of step with dominant Episcopal ideas about visiting and caring for the dying. If we extrapolate from Taylor's to our own time, the lesson is something like this: Introspection and self-examination are natural and appropriate moments in the lives of sick persons. They are moments naturally expressed in the metaphors and liturgy of the church—indeed, moments that should have been focused in this way throughout a lifetime. A priest's communication with someone who is ill must help to make it possible to talk about the "crime(s) of one's life." If the clergy do not help to enable this communication, the inevitable result is dishonesty and isolation—in effect, excommunication.

Community does not end with death. Some responsibilities to the deceased remain. After weeping, Taylor says, we should compose the body, veil it from the curious, then inter it, without ostentation and superstition, negligence or impiety. The funeral should involve no inflated rhetoric or elaborate orations. Once it is done, we owe it to the dead to carry out their will and/or other personal duties, to "right their causes and assert their honor." As we fulfill these charges, we know the dead are aware of our actions, even though we do not know "the mode of their existence."[21]

The American Episcopal Church in effect follows these exhortations. There are no prohibitions on cremation, rubrics advocate burial from the church and require a closed casket, covered with a pall, not flowers. Sermons are the exception rather than the rule. There is a repeated liturgical insistence on the hope of eternal community between the departed and God:

Into your hands, O merciful Savior, we commend your servant N. Acknowledge, we humbly beseech you, a sheep of your own fold, a lamb of your own flock, a sinner of your own redeeming. Receive him/her into the arms of your mercy, into the blessed rest of everlasting peace, and into the glorious company of the saints in light.

O God, whose mercies cannot be numbered: Accept our prayers on behalf of thy servant N., and grant him/her an entrance into the land of light and joy, in the fellowship of thy saints; through Jesus Christ thy Son our Lord, who liveth and reigneth with thee and the Holy Spirit, one God, now and for ever.

The committal of the body or ashes:

All that the Father giveth me shall come to me;
and him that cometh to me I will in no wise cast out.
He that raised up Jesus from the dead
will also give life to our mortal bodies,
by his Spirit that dwelleth in us.

Wherefore my heart is glad, and my spirit rejoiceth;
my flesh also shall rest in hope.
Thou shalt show me the path of life;
in thy presence is the fullness of joy,
and at thy right hand there is pleasure for evermore.

Then, while earth is cast upon the coffin, the celebrant says these words:

> In sure and certain hope of the resurrection to eternal life through our
> Lord Jesus Christ, we commend to Almighty God our brother N; and we
> commit his/her body to the ground;* earth to earth, ashes to ashes, dust to
> dust. The Lord bless him/her and keep him/her, the Lord make his face to
> shine upon him/her and be gracious unto him/her, the Lord lift up his
> countenance upon him/her and give him/her peace.

Thus the tone of the service is one of mixed realism and joy at hope of
new life found beyond death. "The liturgy for the dead is an Easter liturgy.
It finds all its meaning in the resurrection. Because Jesus was raised from
the dead, we too shall be raised."[22]

Hope for the deceased is combined with consolation for the bereaved.
Grieving, solemn and intense mourning are appropriate, but they should
be limited. If the deceased died in the Lord, he is better off, Taylor thought.
And if he did not, he is beyond our hope. In any event, the decedent has
passed beyond reach of our ability to help, out of our hands. We have, he
continues,

> no reason to love the immoderate sorrows of those who too earnestly
> mourn for their dead, when in the last resolution of the enquiry, it is their
> own evil and present or feared inconveniences they deplore: the best that
> can be said of such a grief is, that those mourners love themselves too
> well.[23]

You need worry about your friend no longer, the burial services are telling the bereaved, for he is in God's hands. Accept your grief, live it, but do
not build your life on it, for to do so is egoism and a betrayal of the new life
in the community of accepted suffering revealed in Christ.

Everyone has to come to terms with death and loss; the characteristic
Anglican strategy is to insist that their acceptance or internalization are
the foundations of truth and the origin of community. The pursuit of
health is a sacred quest, when seen in this context. The goal of medicine
should be to encourage health among human beings, and the encourage-
ment of health is different from the avoidance of death. It is a mistake for
medicine and medical practice to take as their ultimate objective the avoidance of death, because in seeking that objective it is seeking to engage a
battle that cannot, indeed should not, be won. Health professionals should
see themselves not as warriors against death but as leaders of the struggle
for health that is but a part of the quest for wholeness.

---

*Or the deep, or the elements, or its resting place.

· 4 ·

Decisions about Death

GENERAL CONSIDERATIONS

In addition to suggesting a perspective on death, Anglican thought leads to some principles that should inform medical decisions about death. Broadly speaking these are principles of loyalty, informed by worship, the past and a cultural tradition. This focus on loyalty makes it important, as we begin to think about specific problems, to separate the crisis or issue itself from our response to it. It is difficult for us to make that distinction. It seems un-American to suggest that there are some problems that can't be solved, but of course there are, at least in the short run; that is immediately clear in the recognition of the inevitablity of suffering. Of course we could "solve" some problems by doing something fundamentally intolerable. For example, the governments of China or India could solve those nations' population problems with a massive campaign of compulsory sterilization, but we believe such a policy would be fundamentally immoral. Our focus, therefore, is not exactly on the problem itself, but on what—in fidelity—we can do about it.

This shift in focus is characteristic of Anglican thought about medical matters. Anglican moral theologians have wanted to see the glory of God in all creation; they have rejoiced in beauty and cried at the hurt and disfigurement they don't understand. But they always work with *a principle of limited liability*—people can't take credit for some of the beautiful things that happen; people can do nothing about some of the bad things.

The immediately relevant manifestation of this tendency is a set of distinctions often used in evaluating care for the dying. Two are especially pertinent: *ordinary* vs. *extraordinary* means of preserving life and *direct* vs. *indirect* killing. Originally the first distinction meant just what it said: Ordinary or routine methods of preserving life (Band-Aids) must be used, extraordinary or esoteric means (heart transplants) need not be used. The idea was that the patient would make the choice, and the moral background was the prohibition on suicide. In any case, modern users of the distinction have tended to relativize it and apply it to the case of *incompetent* patients. They will let *me* decide what is extraordinary for *you*, and they realize that circumstances alter cases. Thus a respirator might be "extraordinary" for one person but "ordinary" for another.

The second traditional distinction, between direct and indirect killing, is based on the idea that any action has multiple consequences, and indirect consequences are not necessarily the responsibility of the agent. For example, if I swerve my car to avoid a child in the road, the death of a cat I happened to strike is not my responsibility or fault. An administrator who discharges an alcoholic employee is not responsible for the results of her subsequent binge, even though it could have been predicted.

Analogously this distinction suggests that palliative care (which may also shorten life) is not the same thing as causing death. A steady escalation of analgesic dosage is tolerable but not injection of an air embolism.

In my opinion these distinctions faithfully reflect important themes in the religious traditions of the West—themes I am about to develop in an Anglican way. The problem with them is that they are somewhat misleading as usually formulated. Thus the ordinary/extraordinary language inevitably suggests it is optional to do any resuscitations, and people who stress direct action tend to correlate our responsibilities too closely to our physical movements, glossing over culpable omissions. Thus I prefer a modified version of this tradition, drawing on the following general considerations:[1]

a. What I do is correctly associated with what I intend. Morality understood as loyalty must refer to our intentions, for loyalty presupposes an intending subject. We might say that the subject matter of morality is not the state of affairs in the world but human responsibility for that state of affairs. There are obviously many things of great human import (natural disasters, seasonal irregularities) for which people are not responsible; many events in which human beings are involved (accidents) are not things for which people are responsible. It is conventional and convenient to associate our responsibilities with our *intentions*.

b. Our intentions have a decisive mental referent. They are inseparable from the conceptual world we inhabit, for our beliefs and theories about reality limit and inform what we can do. One cannot intend something he has no concept of. On the other hand, it is not clear that we intend every foreseen consequence of our actions. Some consequences are so trivial that it would be bizarre to say that we intend them. Thus the rug ruined by bloodstains from a murder victim is inseparable from the killer's purpose, but it would be odd to say that he intended to damage the rug in the same way that he intended his victim's death.

Similarly, some consequences or associated features of an act may be so momentous that we are mistakenly tempted to say that *any* act that precedes those consequences must be of the same moral character as any other. Shooting a kidnapper standing in front of the *Mona Lisa* predictably has the same result for the picture as desecrating it to prevent its theft, but presumably we will look more kindly on the former than on the latter action. This is because destruction of Leonardo's masterpiece is unintentional in the first case in a way it is not in the second.

In the context of our discussion, this point suggests that we must distinguish among acts of care for the dying. Some of these acts intend care—through relief of pain, provision of palliative care and comfort—and simultaneously may shorten life. They differ from acts that intend death. It is not clear that we can produce a hard-and-fast rule that will determine which actions fall into which of these categories, but it is fairly clear that we need to make the distinction. We should realize that there is "a clear distinction to be drawn between rendering someone unconscious at the risk of killing him and killing him in order to render him unconscious."[2] A physician whose patient dies after an increased dosage of a pain-killing drug is not an executioner.

c. At the same time, persons are not entitled to describe their acts in any way they may choose. We rightly describe as insane someone whose descriptions of his or her actions fails to cohere with the perceptions of others who share the same broad view of the world. There is a fine line to be drawn here, to be sure, for a moral reformer is someone who challenges a culture's existing set of descriptions and forces redescription in a new and illuminating way. Still, on the whole, it is reasonable to expect a kind of rough correlation between observable behavior and intentionality. There cannot be many persons in the industrialized world who can turn an ignition key without intending to start the associated motor.

It is important in this context to note that one thing that differentiates various subcultures and traditions within a pluralistic nation-state is the families of action-descriptions they acknowledge. A drunken spree in one context is a good wake in another; suicide can be seen as hara-kiri. Stanley Hauerwas and Gilbert Meilaender have argued with great power that the kind of distinction I propose among forms of care for the dying is only plausible within the context of a community that describes life as a gift from a sovereign God, sees that God as involved in human affairs, and understands life and history to be within his providence. In this context, and only in this context, they suggest, can we make sense of the kind of distinction among acts of care for the dying that I am trying to draw.[3]

While I concede a great deal to this contention, including the idea that there may be peculiar (and powerful) descriptions of care for the dying that are characteristic of our religious communities, Anglicanism, as I argued in chapters 1 and 2, does not admit its sectarian negative implication that the common sensibility of modern persons has no capacity for the distinction. It is found in the common-law tradition, as well as a whole stream of literary, social and political components in our common life. Thus while we might disagree on hard cases, I would expect considerable agreement on the question of whether a given death was intended or not. The community of evaluation in which Anglicanism works is not just the visible religious community but society as a whole.

d. This brings us to the last general point. The actual evaluation of intentional actions will as often proceed by use of symbol and metaphor, analogy and parable as through specification of general and abstract behavioral rules. The basic reason for this method is that our consciousness or intentions are formed by imitation and example, by revolt and protest, by thinking about past and future—rather than on some more mathematical model. Our intentions are formed by our consciousness, which is poetic and metaphorical and is shaped by the experiences of a lifetime. To be sure, we need to make some generalizations about intentions. I do not mean to suggest that these general rules have no place or that they are logically unhelpful. But their place is limited, and moral evaluation has to get at some more primary data.

We now turn to three different kinds of decisions about death that cannot be avoided. These concern impaired newborns, incompetent persons, and competent persons who decide for their own death. I shall treat these situations separately.

NEWBORNS[4]

It is convenient to begin with human beings whose dependency is most obvious, i.e., newborn babies. Increasingly it is clear that there is no area of modern medicine in which the heartache is so great. What does it mean to be faithful to an infant whose prognosis is dismal and at whose suffering we are forced to weep? I will try to spell out some general requirements of fidelity—and to show what these demand, if we think that a baby might be better off dead. Thus I will take five different angles of vision on the problem considering factors of particularity, the future, the body, equality and procedure. I hope the discussion is coherent, but it will be the coherence of a symphony rather than that of a deductive proof.

Particularity

First, when we try to figure out how to take care of someone, we often think about the things they live for, what— as we say—makes them tick. Thus when it comes time to shop for presents for a birthday or Christmas we look for presents that relate to the interests of a person. A set of records of Beethoven is marvelous for one person, a waste for someone else. One person likes jewelry, someone else a set of golf clubs. People's interests or, as I would prefer to say, their loyalties, vary. Taking care of someone means respecting this kind of particularity. And the respect may go quite far; my love for my friend may well bring me to love what he loves, to care for those things that matter to him.

Usually we know something of a person's specificity from his or her explicitly stated preferences. We know that Dad likes to play golf because he says he does, and he says he doesn't care for classical music. In fact, however, this correlation between what people really are and who or what they *say* they are is not one to one. Many people *say* they like to do things which in fact it is clear that they do not much enjoy; anyone who has ever lived in a family can write a book about the various kinds of self-deception that human beings indulge in. Still, throughout most of our lives, we are willing to acknowledge that a person's decisions about his or her own life ought to have a preferred place. Medical decisions are no exception. Thus loyalty supports a right to refuse treatment and a stress on the importance of a requirement of informed consent.

The striking thing about severely impaired babies is that this aspect of moral consideration simply does not exist for them. They have never had a chance to care about or live for anything. They have not established a style of life or character. It's not just that because of great defect they will never have the kind of personality that a normal person would have; it's rather that they have never got off the launching pad. The effect on our moral reasoning about them is that an important variable simply drops out of the picture.

In order to see the effect of this difference, it is important to note another dimension of these infants' lives. They begin with no medical history beyond what may have been learned through antenatal diagnosis. Their prognosis is at best uncertain. We don't know how retarded a child with Down's syndrome will be or how serious the impairment associated with myelomeningocele will turn out to be. Some premature babies have terrible and short lives; others do not. It is never possible to be absolutely sure of the outcome.

I draw from these facts the conclusion that for the most part we owe it to these babies to get them started. I realize that there are strong arguments against this conclusion. It is much harder to disconnect the respirator than it is never to turn it on. I do not wish to dismiss this feeling as irrelevant, only to note that it must be compromised somewhat if we are really to respect the particularity of the baby. I will return to this issue later. For the moment I simply want to stress two things: The kinds of personal style and preference arguments that may justify a decision for the death of an adult can never be applied directly to newborns, and it takes time to establish a pattern of biological functioning that we can extrapolate to future events and responses with some degree of plausibility.

Future

A second thing that loyalty to another person means is interest in or concern for what he or she may become. This idea is difficult perhaps. We tend to form set pictures of people—"Oh, he could do it if he wanted to, but he will never skip Monday night football." We think of people as set in their ways: *He* is punctual, *she* is stubborn, *they* are argumentative. It is true that people's characters have a kind of constancy, but it is also true that people change and grow. Saints fall away, sinners convert, Prince Hal becomes Henry IV.

When we look into the future for our friends, we find that we want many things for them. One of these is *happiness*. This term is notoriously hard to define, and I am not capable of producing a statement that will instantly persuade everyone. But it is obvious that happiness is something that we want for those that we care about. We would describe as *sick* someone who wanted his child or spouse or parents to be *un*happy. Naturally I don't mean that we want happiness of any kind for them—we may well feel that some kinds of happiness are better than others. But, all else being equal, we prefer that our friends be happy rather than not.

A second thing that we want for our friends is *excellence*. We hope that they will do something well. This something may be athletic, intellectual or social. Some are good runners, others good thinkers, others are, as we say, good people. However we may define it, excellence is something that we want for our friends.

Given these goals, the question becomes whether they are attainable. Seldom do we know the answer, particularly with handicapped babies. We may be certain that they will *not* have the kinds of happiness or excellence that are open to normal children, *but that is scarcely the issue*. We are not trying to compare them with others. Who of us would survive some great assize trying to decide if his life, with all its defects, was worth living? The issue is, is some kind of happiness or excellence open to this child? We are the custodians of their future, and we should act with hope.

Body

Third, loyal care for persons involves care for their bodies. Human beings are not just personalities nor bundles of potentiality; they are also living, struggling bodies. There are two aspects of this obvious point to which I wish to call attention. One of them is that the body has a kind of life of its own. It is not altogether malleable to human desire, whether we speak of the desire of its "owner" or of someone else. And health is comparably objective.

Let me put the issue a little differently. Bodies are not just things we have, they are things we *are*. The requirements of a healthy body can be generalized—they are not just relative to cultural prejudices or values. And medical care involves care for bodies in a special way. Not to the exclusion of everything else. Not only in a scientific way that excludes the caress and the cuddle—but oriented to the body all the same. My lawyer is a consultant on my rights, my tax man on my money and my doctor on my body and its health.

Secondly, an important feature of bodies is that they change. Bodies pass through stages, regardless of the desires of anyone. These include infancy, adolescence, middle age, aging and dying. Proper forms of care should be adjusted to these various stages or moments in a life span. Pediatrics is not just medicine on small adults; we use different terms to describe a highway accident to children, other adults and the aged. Fidelity to a patient will always require optimal care, but as we change, so do the requirements of care. The central fact is that human needs change. Throughout most of our lives medical loyalty to us means keeping us alive, but this goal ceases to be valid at some point in our lives. Then we may actually speak of a need to die. Dr. Anna Fletcher has referred to a baby who was "trying to die."

Paul Ramsey has made this point with characteristic force. He says that the determination of when a person enters dying is a "medical" decision, meaning that changes in the ill person himself determine what the right forms of treatment are. When a person starts to die, then our responsibilities shift. It is easy to confuse this claim with another: that some dying lives are not worth living. But that second idea presupposes a *comparison* with a hypothesized form of the life worth living. Ramsey's idea, which Anglicanism should endorse, is that a person's life trajectory at some point enters a dying phase. When that happens, moral responsibility changes. The issue is not,

"Is his life worth living?" We have no way to answer such a question. The issue is, "Is he dying?" or—more generally—"What forms of treatment are optimal care for him in whatever time he has left?"

If the determination of when someone begins to die—a determination that is relevant to the choice of appropriate forms of care—is a matter of what Eric Cassell has called the "healer's art," the substance of the point is best captured not in argument but in metaphor. A couple invite friends to dinner. Food and drink are pleasant; the conversation bubbles. The good host is hospitable and courteous to his guest, no matter what his shifts in mood. But there comes a time when the party "winds down"—a time to acknowledge that the evening is over. At that point, not easily determined by clock, conversation or basal metabolism, the good host does not press his guest to stay but lets him go. Indeed he may have to signal that it is acceptable to leave. A good host will never be sure of his timing and will never kick out his guest. His jurisdiction over the guest is limited to taking care and permitting departure.

Analogously, loyalty to other persons involves care for them of the best possible sort, and changing the forms of care as needs change. It means recognizing that a time comes when we can care for them no longer, only bid them Godspeed. We may, as it were, show them the door. But we should not kill a patient, because that would be to betray him, to assume the kind of jurisdiction over his fate that is incompatible with being a good host. And we can never be sure of our timing.

Loyalty to the dying at some point requires a choice of palliative clinical care and personal human support over life-extending technologies. It is of the greatest possible importance that this shift be seen as a shift to an alternative *medical* form of care, and it is the great strength of the hospice movement to have refined and institutionalized these alternative forms of medical care. Loyalty to the dying not only tolerates but positively mandates this shift; making a guest stay longer than is good for him is very bad manners.

In effect, I am suggesting that some children are born dying. Thus I think we should let some newborns die. On the other hand, predictable impairment, in particular retardation, is not a sufficient reason for saying a child is dying. It is especially important not to yield to pressure to come to a quick and efficient decision in order to spare people's feelings. It takes time to discern what is going on with a young patient's small body.

Equality

Fourth, because we have many loyalties we need a principle to appeal to when they conflict—as they often do. Equality is a valuable guideline for these purposes. A commitment to equal treatment serves to protect the defective newborn from invidious comparisons. It is tempting to contrast her prospects with those of normal children or to suggest that she deserves something other than the optimal treatment available. The principle of equality calls in question quality of life as a criterion for triage.

At the same time, equality also limits. Our equal commitment to all children means we cannot have unlimited involvements with anyone. Unlimited loyalties tend to become idolatries. We owe special and different but not exactly *more* care to a handicapped baby. This factor is a hard one to weigh into our calculations. I do not mean that as persons or institutions we ought always to be balancing one claim against another. Rather, I mean that as we organize our personal or collective lives we need to build in some checks and balances. It is good if parents have another child, or a job they love, and if staff and doctors realize that they are needed elsewhere as well.

Procedure

This brings us to the last point I wish to make. Loyalty to an impaired baby requires involvement in a decision-making procedure of integrity and credibility.

Some writers on medical ethics see this as the only issue. In the case of adults they stress the patient's right to die; for children they assert an absolute right of parents to make the decision. It is not clear, however, that the gift of a child entitles parents to unlimited sovereignty over it. Even if they are the child's best proxy in virtue of their identification with it, their power should not be unchecked. There are various reasons for this conclusion, but two suffice. One is the finitude of parental judgment and the possibility that their identification and stake in the issue will produce excessive bias. The other is the social nature of human existence that I have stressed. We do not live by ourselves; the family is not an island. Desertion of the family —and simply leaving the decision in their hands may amount to desertion —is a form of betrayal.

In effect I am saying that loyalty in these situations requires the virtue Jeremy Taylor stresses before death: patience. There is no rushing the decision-making procedure and no substitute for involvement of the physician throughout it. What is needed is lots of talking among parents, physicians, nurses and appropriately concerned others.

This is no panacea. Even a good process can go wrong or be misused. I can well understand the impulse to establish minimal standards in the law, for in this area discretion abused is not just indiscreet; it is immoral. I do not think babies should be let go simply by virtue of Down's syndrome—as

I hope I have suggested. But I cannot imagine a regulatory net or law that would ensure right results or could be fine-tuned to all the variety of cases we want to acknowledge. Thus I fall back on moral education and a process of listening, learning and support.

In sum: Loyalty is what we owe a defective baby. We owe her respect and hope, care and comfort for her body, fair play and due process. Sometimes this will mean we have to kiss her good-bye, but never without having made her welcome, never without a hug and never without regret.

OLDER PERSONS WHO CAN'T DECIDE FOR THEMSELVES

Under this heading I wish to consider the criteria we should appeal to when we consider choosing death for noninfants who have never expressed preferences, or whose wishes it seems plausible to discount. My strategy will be to outline four different proposals about when a decision for their deaths should be made. I will characterize and illustrate these options and then turn to offer a sketch of a fifth proposal that, with all its limits, I find more adequate than the four with which I shall begin.

Usual Medical Practice

The traditional criterion for making decisions is the standard of what is *usually medically done*. The right thing to do is what physicians in a particular community usually do. This standard controlled in American law until only recently. For example, in the first decision about Karen Quinlan,[5] a New Jersey court held that Ms. Quinlan's father, Joseph, should not be made her guardian and be allowed to authorize disconnection of her respirator, because it was usual medical practice in the state of New Jersey not to allow that to be done. The court held that this was a medical decision and as such was rightly controlled by usual medical practice. Since doctors usually continued to resuscitate patients in Ms. Quinlan's circumstances, they should continue to resuscitate her.

Adopting this kind of standard offers some important advantages. We can see one of them if we think of other kinds of managerial decisions we all make. One role I once played was that of departmental chairman. When confronted with a departmental crisis, my first impulse was to ask either what my *predecessor* did in a similar situation, or what *other* chairmen who might face a similar problem would do under the circumstances. In other words I asked about precedent and customary practice. Often the result was very specific and helpful guidance about what I should do. We learn from example, and there is, so to speak, safety in numbers. Furthermore, the standard of usual medical care is comparatively objective. It pushes against idiosyncratic choices, made simply on the basis of my own impulses, emotions or feelings and toward doing what is plausible and defensible in the eyes of a knowledgeable group of people. Finally, it is probably protective of life. In a culture with our value heritage, the fact that standards have to be public standards everyone would use, pushes toward standards that will protect human beings when they are weak, poor or crippled. There is a lot to be said for the usual medical-care standard, and it has obvious attractions for an Anglican sensibility.

On the other hand, it has some problems. Its value decreases as consensus breaks down. If it is impossible to say what is usually done, then it doesn't do us any good to appeal to what is usually done as a way of solving a problem. It is one thing to appeal to a standard when there is a consensus; if there is no consensus, then attempting to appeal to it is circular. And, as a matter of fact, there is extraordinary diversity among health professionals about the right way to treat people when we all wonder whether they should go on living.

The medical-care theory may in fact be too conservative. As a practical matter it may have the effect that no one is ever let go, because we are always going to be able to find precedent for a decision to continue care. Of course it is not necessarily wrong to be conservative, but to avoid begging the question we need to entertain the possibility that there are some times when people should be allowed to die. This theory may foreclose that possibility.

Finally, this theory may not sufficiently take into account value differences among physicians, on the one hand, and patients, on the other. The strategy we are discussing—accept death when it is usually accepted—tends to gloss over the pluralism of values in our society and the important fact that at this time of all times people may have a case for being judge in their own cause. Therefore the next option comes up:

Patient's Prior Judgment
In the second general strategy for deciding about death, the correct judgment to make is the *prior judgment* of the *patient*. What should we do? We should do what the patient told us ahead of time to do. It is important in assessing this option to acknowledge that its defenders mean to refer not to a casual statement of an individual but to his or her considered judgment. Karen Quinlan was reported to have remarked that she never wanted to be a vegetable. The New Jersey courts rightly refused to base a judgment about ongoing care for Ms. Quinlan on those remarks, for it would have

been implausible to conclude that they represented a thought-out and serious judgment made by her.[5]

On the other hand, in another well-known case, a court did take with the greatest possible seriousness earlier judgments made by the patient. Brother Fox, a Roman Catholic monk, had repeatedly and most clearly expressed his conviction that he did not want extraordinary means of care used on him in his last days. Later, while working in the garden of his religious community, Brother Fox suffered a hernia. During his operation he experienced cardiac arrest and, although he was resuscitated, a period of anoxia occurred sufficient to cause brain damage. He became permanently comatose. His Brothers in his religious order went to court to ask that he be taken off the respirator, and they won. For our purposes the thing to note is the reason for the court's judgment: It acknowledged a prior judgment by Brother Fox, a judgment supported by his life commitments, which embodied the same style of life that the judgment reflected.[6]

In assessing this method of making decisions about life and death we find it to be the mirror image of the viewpoint I tried to discuss initially. This perspective begins with a conviction about the value of individual self-determination, an assumption that different people treasure different values and live for different things. It is a consumer perspective, if the one I initially discussed can be described as a managerial one. Thus it is characteristically the point of view of persons who have reason to worry about other people taking over their lives. It is a viewpoint that is extraordinarily important in the United States which, after all, began with the Declaration of Independence.

Nevertheless, this point of view has some serious problems. The first of these arises if we ask questions like: "What counts as a judgment?" "Must it be in writing?" "How old do you have to be?" "Must it be made in a situation free from duress?" Related are issues about changes of mind. Many of us have made judgments at one time that we later have had to question, if not positively to eat. To follow a person's prior judgment in a matter as consequential as a decision to die, we ought to be reassured that it represents his or her continuing conviction.

Furthermore, what are we going to do about what many of us would think of as bizarre choices? I think of the athlete who is said to live for his sport. Suppose someone feels that, if he can no longer play baseball, his life is not worth living. Would we then want to accede to a request for termination of treatment rather than amputation of a leg? The general issue is that people can be mistaken about themselves. That someone may wish not to live in certain circumstances cannot be denied, but does it follow that death is in their interest?

It is a doctor's business to know why [a patient] wishes to die, and to serve
the patient's interests by going to the root of the wish. To a clinical psychi-
atrist, the human instinct to live is so basic that a wish to die *must* be a
sign of disorder, of pathological depression—a condition to be treated, if
possible, and cured.[7]

This statement may go too far, but it rightly raises the issue of the complex
motivations of persons, with the related moral problem for bystanders.
Which part of the patient's self is the real self? Aged and dependent people,
Dunstan observes, are ambivalent—they neither want to die nor to be a
nuisance. Impatience by those taking care may suggest that others don't
want to bother with them any longer. Patients should be protected from
these conflicts of interest, and family and medical staff should not live in a
context of possible abuse, suspicion and fear.

A final problem that arises with this point of view concerns our response
in circumstances in which no choice has been expressed. Some critics of this
proposal notice that, if we took it seriously, we might be forced to infer
conservative practices about continuing treatment for people who have
not explicitly requested that treatment be discontinued. That would be terrible, for many of those people have not really decided they want a lengthy
treatment. They have simply not wanted to come to terms with the issue.
There always will be many cases where a prior judgment of a patient either
cannot be or has not been expressed, and this theory provides us with no
help or guidance in those cases.

Thus I conclude: While a prior judgment by a patient may be of considerable relevance in many circumstances and the preferences of a patient
are never irrelevant, still this standard does not offer a *sufficient* resolution
of our problems.

Reasonable Person

In the third and fourth options the general idea is that someone else puts
herself in the patient's place and then decides what to do under the circumstances. Thus these views are usually described as substitute, or substituted
judgment. One person's judgment is substituted for that of another. A family member, a physician, an attorney—some competent person's—judgment is substituted for that of the patient who, it is assumed, is in no position
to judge for himself or herself. Under the notion of substituted judgment,
however, we find two very different emphases.

The first of these can be described as the *reasonable-person* standard.
Here the basic question we ask in making a treatment decision is, "Is it reasonable to go on living under these circumstances?" This was the court's
standard in a Massachusetts case involving an unfortunate man named

Joseph Saikewicz.[8] Mr. Saikewicz was profoundly retarded. He had lived his entire life in the Belchertown School, a Massachusetts institution for the mentally infirm. At age sixty-six he developed an acute form of leukemia. Persons responsible for Saikewicz's care were uncertain what to do. There was no hope, they thought, of curing his leukemia. He would not understand the treatments required for the disease, so the various discomforts to which he would be subjected—injections, nausea, and hair loss associated with chemotherapy—would terrify him. He would have to be tied down to be treated. Uncertain that this forecast was something that really was in Saikewicz's interest, some of the staff at the Belchertown School went to court to ask permission not to treat. Their fundamental argument was that it would be unreasonable to choose a course of treatment that could only be terrifying, frightening, and from which there was no plausible hope of success. They won.

This verdict illustrates certain characteristics of the reasonable-person standard. When asked to describe what counts as being reasonable or unreasonable, its defenders usually suggest that it is unreasonable to want to endure pain or to want to continue to exist while unconscious. They thus develop a concept related to reasonableness, and that is the concept of interest. They suggest that it is unreasonable to want to go against one's interest and that all persons have an interest in being aware and avoiding pain.

Two further features of the reasonable-person standard should be discussed. Note that there are some kinds of medical situations and some patients for whom the only possible substituted judgment is of the reasonable-person sort. Newborn babies, as I have observed, have never established a mode of being in the world. It makes no sense to speak of their personalities, their hopes, their dreams or their fears. Thus, if we try to make a substituted judgment for them, the judgment we make will have to be some sort of version of the reasonable-person standard. It is not possible in their case to extrapolate from a past life or to guess the effect of what they would have done. We could, if we wanted to, try to make that extrapolation in the case of Joseph Saikewicz, but we cannot reason in that way in the case of an impaired newborn.

This brings me to the second feature of the reasonable-person standard to which I wish to call attention. The Saikewicz case aroused a great deal of controversy, most of it revolving around two points. One has to do with the mental gymnastics involved in a rational, competent adult attempting to determine what is irrational for a mentally retarded person to want. Certainly there are some problems associated with this intellectual maneuver.

On the other hand, the Saikewicz decision raises another controversial point, and that point relates to the court's conclusion about *who* should make these decisions. The Saikewicz court held that decisions about termination of life support should be made by a court of law. The court's holding is based in part on a grasp of the magnitude and seriousness of the issues at stake. The court felt that just as we don't allow death sentences to be passed without the approval of a court, so we shouldn't allow other decisions for death to be made without the thorough procedural control and objectivity that are associated with the judicial system.

This stress on judicial decision-making in the Saikewicz case is totally coherent with the court's ruling that the appropriate frame of reference is the reasonable-person standard. For if we ask where a reasonable person is to be found, the plausible answer is: in someone who is *removed* from the situation at hand. If we want an objective decision, we characteristically go to a *neutral* third party, and that is precisely the role played by courts. If reasonableness and objectivity go together, as they seem to in the mind of the Saikewicz court, then it is absolutely plausible to suggest that the best social location for decision-making power is in the judicial system.

Actual Person

This brings us to the fourth criterion to which people sometimes appeal when they attempt to make decisions about death. It is another form of substituted judgment, and we will call it an *actual*-person standard. Under the actual-person standard the question we ask ourselves is, "What *would* Tom have chosen for himself?" We extrapolate from the values, lifestyle and character of the particular patient to a decision or conclusion that is coherent with that particularity. We are making an inference based on visible and social data. This reasoning is the kind I referred to when I described decisions about defective babies. It is exactly the sort of reasoning one cannot use about a baby, since the baby has not had any chance to set down tracks from which we can plausiby guess the course he or she might choose for himself or herself.

This view of substituted judgment involves a somewhat more dramatic shift or transposition of ourselves into the patient's psyche. In the first case we are asking ourselves what would have been *reasonable* for someone to have done. In this case we are asking what would they *really* have done. The difference in the questions is, of course, important, and the fact that creates the difference is that few persons are always fully rational people. What a *rational* person should do and what *any one specific* person would do are not necessarily or perhaps even frequently the same thing.

This version of the actual-person standard of substituted judgment has found a home in American law. Specifically it is the rule in the second and final New Jersey court decision in the Quinlan case.[9] The higher court held that judgments about her treatment should reflect her actual life, choices she had actually made, and therefore should be made by someone who knew her well, in this case her father. Joseph Quinlan was given authority to order disconnection of her respirator, and the respirator was disconnected. (Karen Quinlan, nevertheless, survived for more than ten years.)

This brings me to the major characteristic of the second version of substituted judgment to which I wish to call attention: It plausibly is associated with the notion that the right decision-maker is not a court but the family. If we are attempting to figure out *not* what someone should *reasonably* have done, *but* what she would *really* have done, then the best decision-maker is not someone who is objective and dispassionate, but someone who knew her very well, and that is of course most plausibly—and without meaning to gloss over all sorts of ambiguities—her family.

Individual Medical Care

In one or the other of the forms I have just tried to describe, substituted judgment seems to be a dominant standard today in American law. I hope I have said enough to suggest why it is plausible, and in many ways good, that these forms of substituted judgment have come to the fore. There are important disagreements about them, to be sure, but each of them in its own way marks an improvement over either an appeal to what is usually medically done, or a simplistic invocation of individual self-determination.

Nevertheless, the substituted-judgment standards as they have been formulated so far present serious problems. First, both versions of substituted judgment are procedurally clumsy. If we say that the family must make the decisions, we have to reckon with the fact that families no longer live together very closely. Thus we may be in the business of trying to hunt up family on the long-distance phone or waiting for people to fly in; decisions are going to be delayed while we try to reach the family. Furthermore, not everyone lives in a family, and we will need some sort of social mechanism to handle decision-making about those persons who are really not known well by anyone.

This procedural clumsiness is, if possible, more acute in the first or reasonable-person version of substituted judgment. We must see that the standard means what it says: It means that before treatment of an individual can be discontinued, a judicial judgment, a court order, must be procured.

I hope I am naïve, but I think I am not, if I suggest that the necessity to procure such court orders would hopelessly complicate the care of gravely ill persons. An inevitable result of this requirement of a court order would be that many people would continue to be treated longer than is reasonable. In other words, the plausible political implementation of a reasonable-person standard tends to interfere with the objective that the standard seeks.

Secondly, substituted judgment is extraordinarily uncertain in its results. It is in no way a standard certain to lead to an objectively "right" answer. This is clear enough in the case of the courts. Not all judges think the same decisions are reasonable, a fact which must be notorious to anyone who has done even a small amount of reading in recent case law on death and dying. But if disagreements occur within the judiciary, these disagreements increase geometrically when we turn to the family. Families, especially families confronted by death, do not always speak with one voice. Luther called the family the school for character, and one reason he used that phrase was his realization that disagreements within families were so heartfelt and so enduring that the development of a capacity to live with disagreement was fostered better in the family than anywhere else. These disagreements are intensified a hundredfold when individual family members are frightened, guilt ridden, concerned about inheritance, and in every other way vexed and perplexed by an impending death. Thus appeal to court or to family is not certain to produce a rational or plausible outcome.

Finally, these forms of substituted judgment obviously have the effect of radically displacing a medical judgment. This displacement is socially and politically understandable. It rests on abuses of medical power both real and imagined. A good deal of medical ethics takes this as its central theme, suggesting that a tyranny of the medical profession is the worst evil to be avoided. I have discussed the general question of power-sharing in chapter 2, and here simply I note that there is something odd about systems of decision-making that have the effect of rendering irrelevant the judgments of those persons most knowledgeable about the facts.

Nor is our intuitive reaction to this situation groundless. Health professionals in general, and physicians in particular, acquire knowledge about the body. This knowledge is *not* a *sufficient* basis for medical decision-making but it is an important ingredient in that decision-making, and theories that make it irrelevant, as the substituted-judgment theories seem to do, are problematical. Thus I think we turn and look for another alternative that I will call an *individual medical-care standard*. Although it leaves hard questions unanswered, it is nowhere written that ethics and theology have as part of their responsibility the elimination of all ambiguity and uncertainty. The trick is to leave the uncertainty in the right place.

As in the case of newborns, I begin with the assumption that the fundamental responsibility of persons is to be loyal and/or faithful to each other, and that medicine always requires care for the body on the part of the physician or other health professionals. Throughout most of the human lifetime medical care requires work toward the cure of disease. But we should remember that the physician has other responsibilities besides cure. Palliative care is provided, or at the very least prescribed, by health professionals. Paul Ramsey sounds a very Anglican theme when he insists that a fundamental need near the end of life is a need for company, a need not to be alone.[10]

Thus, as I suggested earlier, the question that should be asked in deciding on forms of care is not "What can he do?" or "Is her life worth living any longer?" Those are not questions we can answer. The only way we could attempt to answer would be to construct a description of an ideal life, or at least an adequate life, and to measure the ill person against that standard. I know no plausible way to engage in the necessary construction of an adequate or an ideal life. The question that we need to ask ourselves is, "*Has this person started dying?*" Is this a life that has entered its last stages?

Although this decision (whether the person is dying) has essential medical components, it is not purely a biological or a physiological decision. That is, it is a matter of discernment, of knowing the patient in the context of his or her world. Thus, in order to decide whether a given person is dying, it is important to know something of the person's history, family, and in the case of adults something of the values for which the person stood.

Most particularly, the discernment that has to be made in the case of a Joseph Saikewicz is whether a given form of treatment will be received as cure, torture or discipline. For most adults, most of the time, painful and inconvenient treatments are seen to be forms of cure; for all of us as children and for some persons all the time some medical interventions are discipline—undergone but not understood for the sake of the future. Some interventions, however, are torture. If the discomfort is severe, the likelihood of success small and the probability of comprehension slim, these facts tend to shift a treatment out of the category of discipline and into that of torture. Sometimes we may be able to say that life-sustaining treatment falls under that heading. If so, it should be abandoned for other forms of care. On a layman's reading of the record I should say that Joseph Saikewicz's was such a case.

I do not mean to suggest that Saikewicz should have been "allowed to die" because he was severely retarded or in his sixties, but I do insist that the patient's perception of a treatment is relevant to the morality of that treatment, and it is clear that Saikewicz would only have been tortured by his treatment. Once an individual has established some particularity, that must be taken into account in figuring out what medical fidelity to him means.

This breadth is important, for it means that if we ask ourselves *who* should make the decision, the only appropriate answer, is "*We* should make the decision." Solitary decision-making by a physician who knows nothing about a patient except his body is as likely to be wrong as a decision by a court far removed from any contact with the actual circumstances, or a decision by a family engulfed by grief and guilt. All those parties should have input into the decision-making process. But because the process has a medical focus it is important that medical expertise be central in it. Thus the decision-making process should be collaborative and collegial, and at its center should be a physician who asks, "Has this person begun to die, is he trying to die, does he have a need to die now?"

CHOOSING MY DEATH

Finally, we come to consider a choice of death for ourselves or our responsibilities and loyalties to and for other persons who choose death. This issue is often discussed under the general heading of "the right to die," but "once the individual's right to die has been conceded . . . it becomes necessary to show that society has an overriding interest in the preservation of this individual's life if the choice is to be interfered with."[11] Exactly what the phrase "right to die" means, moreover, is quite vague. At its most crisp, it would suggest that physicians must kill seriously ill patients on order, but not all its advocates are so clear.

In any case, the fact of patient choice or consent is not a sufficient justification for deciding for death; the "moral status" of a choice for death "is determined by those circumstances which make the act what it is."[12] We cannot assume that any choice for death must be respected but must confront the substantive issue that remains: Conceding as I did in chapter 3 the importance of accepting death, when *should* death be chosen? Within the Anglican tradition it is clear that the loneliness, meaninglessness, frustration, pain, futility or brokenness of someone's life are in themselves insufficient reasons for the choice of death. For our very selves are social, and one cannot resign from life without profound repercussions. *Accepting* despair and the humiliation of impoverished and weakened life may often be a great contribution to the moral health of the community—and it is much more likely to be so than speedy, efficient departure once "productiveness" is over.

In any context suicide is a social act, the unanswerable nonverbal gesture in a social dialogue. There is no doubt at all that good reasons can be advanced for it in particular cases of great pain, and it has been defended in this century by thoughtful Anglicans like Dean Inge and Joseph Fletcher. They find it consistent with stress on rational personality and a utilitarian calculation of social needs. But because selfhood is so social, suicide cannot be simply a matter of private right.

This sociality has two dimensions. One is theological. As a child of God the Christian must relate all choices to that relationship. Thus

> . . . the actual claims of other human beings are not the only claims that the Christian has to consider. Even were their interests in no way impaired by what he had in mind to do, he would still feel that he was not absolutely free to do whatever he wished. Consequently he can claim no inalienable right to death on the grounds that his life is his own. . .[13]

Why not? Because his life belongs to God. Theology in the sense of beliefs about God makes a difference in reasoning about suicide or voluntary euthanasia.

At the same time relations to other human beings are relevant. It is easy to imagine medical circumstances in which it appears that everyone would be better off if I were to take my own life. And it is impossible to say that this action should *never* be required by loyalty. But the great difficulty with supposed altruistic suicide, on medical grounds, is that it ignores the guilt felt by others and the desertion of them that is involved. "Might not the person for whose sake I am prepared to take my own life say to me that there are some burdens, even 'intolerable burdens' which he would rather not do without if the only alternative is to be relieved of them by suicide?"[14] To be sure, one can always claim that in his case these factors do not apply. But one can never be sure, and suicide is an irrevocable act.

The great moral danger of medical suicide is that it will be egotistical and manipulative, symbolic of an unwillingness to play the role of dependent when it falls to our turn. Theologically it may "be the expression of a refusal to trust in God, an embracing of death for its own sake, a form of self-justification, a desertion to the enemy." Indeed, as Peter Baelz contends:

It might be argued that, if death ought for the Christian to be a passion, something that he undergoes in utter dependence on God, then suicide and voluntary euthanasia, which make of death an action, something deliberately encompassed by man himself, even if it is performed at the hand of another, is *ipso facto* wrong, whether it expresses a deliberate rejection of God or not.[15]

Along these same lines Taylor claimed centuries ago that persons should not presume to choose their cause of death as "all such nicety of choice is nothing but a colour or impatience," although we may beg of God that our sickness be not "sharp or noisome, infectious or unusual." As we contemplate our death, he contends, we should remember its inevitability, remain faithful to the best in our past and make the best of the situation. (We should not try to be too religious, for we will fail.) And we should do what the doctor tells us without "uncivil distrustings or refusing his prescriptions upon humors or impatient fear." Physicians are instruments of God who "enables their judgments and prospers their medicines" insofar as they are effective. Nurses are to be treated well "as it becomes an obliged and necessitous person." Thus, one should not call for death, "but wherever the general hath placed thee, stir not from thy station until thou beest called off; but abide so, that death may come to thee by the design of him who intends it to be thy advantage."

This is a vision of life which is to be lived through to an end in dependence. It does not imply that one has to go on as long as possible:

A man may refuse to have his arm or leg cut off ... and if he believes that to die is the less evil, he may compose himself to it without hazarding his patience.... When there is reason they should decline him [i.e., the doctor's services], it is not to be accounted to the stock of sin; but where there is no just cause, there is a direct impatience.[16]

Far from wanting the relatively clean and efficient end of life that suicide entails, Taylor thought that infirmity and leisurely dying had their advantages. Sudden death was preferable only if one happened to be "caught in the state and exercise of virtue." And one should be grateful for a time when appropriately abbreviated prayers and religious images could be the focus of attention.[17]

In addition to these relational considerations, Anglican arguments against medically indicated taking of one's own life include some practical arguments. Patients requesting death may change their minds; "those who are left are often full of recrimination, guilt and anger"; uncertainties in diagnosis and prognosis are inevitable; the social context that makes the decision for death plausible may change; to engage in killing is inconsistent with the physician's conventional role, and trust between physicians and patients will be undermined.[18]

The core thread, however, is the idea that "medically indicated" suicide represents a desertion or betrayal of others and an impatient assertion of the self against conditions of finitude that are part of embodied existence.

> Men exercise and achieve their humanity in interdependence. There is a movement of giving and receiving. . . . In the giver it demands unlimited caring, in the recipient absolute trust. The question must be asked whether the practice of voluntary euthanasia is consistent with the fostering of such caring and trust.[19]

From the Anglican viewpoint the individualism that voluntary euthanasia represents is a mistaken interpretation of reality.

The mistake, moreover, is not strictly intellectual, for in a real community conventions must nurture care and trust. Proposals to *legalize* voluntary euthanasia are fundamentally pitiless:

> We can discuss euthanasia with rational detachment in the lecture room or the club, in enjoyment of our health. But in sickness, when vitality is low, rationality is weakened; our biological instinct to survive, to protect ourselves, throws up fears and fantasies. At present the syringe, the tablet or the draught in the hand of the nurse spells comfort if not cure. But once legislation has created the possibility that these were instruments of death, confidence would have gone; rationality alone would not protect us from even groundless fear. There are exceptions, calm, steady men. But life cannot be organized on the supposition that every man is a Socrates. We need, as we now have, a complex of expectations, conventions, rituals, sanctions professional and legal, to maintain our interest in a basic social confidence that life is precious and is normally to be protected. We are not without the instinct with which birds and animals defend life; but those instincts are weakened in us. We support them in these other, rational, typically human ways. They protect, not simply the lives of men but also the humanity of man. This is why we should not ask our doctors to put us or our kind to death.[20]

Rather than voluntary euthanasia, Anglicanism should support organizations like the Samaritans[21] and hospices. In the United States this support should be even more forthright than it is already. Commitment to effective symptom control, interdisciplinary care, provision of communal support for patient and family through dying and bereavement, befriending those who are alone: These are the goals of hospices and Samaritans. It is hard to imagine forms of medical care more congruent with the general emphasis of this book.[22]

· 5 ·

Sexuality and New Life

The marriage service in the American *Book of Common Prayer* begins
with an exhortation that includes these words:

> The union of husband and wife in heart, body and mind is intended by
> God for their mutual joy; for the help and comfort given one another in
> prosperity and adversity; and, when it is God's will, for the procreation
> of children and their nurture in the knowledge and love of the Lord.[1]

These are traditional "goods" or "ends" of marriage, variously formulated in Christian tradition over the past 1,500 years or more. They do not
stress the idea of marriage as a remedy for sin, nor has that purpose ever
been emphasized in the American prayer book exhortation.[2] Rather, they
suggest that sexuality is a cause for rejoicing, not a curse, that it remedies
sin by providing a fundamental form of companionship among persons,
and that it relates to the beginning of human life.

The statement's objectivity is striking. The union "is intended by God"
for "mutual joy . . . help and comfort . . . and, when it is God's will, for the
procreation of children"; these are not exactly optional components of the
relationship that the couple may choose or reject. Moreover, the couple is
not isolated in their affirmations. After they have repeated their free con-
sents the celebrant turns to the congregation and asks,

> Will all of you witnessing these promises do all in your power to uphold
> these two persons in their marriage?

To which the appropriate answer is "We will."[3] Naturally "the role of
family, friends and the community, which is often crucial in sustaining or
breaking a marriage, is openly recognized" in this exchange,[4] and the as-
sembled group as a whole is caught up in a collective affirmation of the
commitments that are being made.

Developments in modern biology, medicine and society raise issues bearing on question of sexual community and procreation. Like most branches of

Christianity, the Anglican Church has greatly modified its views on women. To be sure, some ambivalence has always existed. Hooker thought women were formed "not only after [males] in time but inferior in excellency," but the perceptible differences "in so due and sweet proportion" were not, for him, easy to conceptualize or define. He noticed differences, he retained a hierarchical idea of the relations of the sexes, but he was reluctant to generalize about or to make an ideology of kinds of superiority or inferiority. Love, "the perfected ground of wedlock," also "is seldom able to yield any reason of itself."[5] Hooker reveals a sense of the mystery in the relation of men and women that keeps him from being unequivocally hierarchical, but this is only a qualification, for the changes in emphasis in ritual and thought over the past three hundred or more years are obvious. Certainly the marriage ritual of the contemporary Episcopal Church means to be egalitarian between women and men.[6]

Important as this issue is, it is not central to the complex of *medically* related problems associated with sexuality that we must take up. Broadly speaking there are two complexes of these: One set concerns the relationship between nature or biological gender and marriage; the others have to do with reproduction.

BIOLOGY AND MARRIAGE

Clearly the marriage ceremony presupposes that the persons involved are biologically male and female. This assumption raises an issue today. Is the possibility of marital community affected by biology? Are these natural constraints that the church must respect? One issue concerns the marriage of homosexual lovers; another those whose genitals have been altered through medical procedures. Is marriage rightly limited to heterosexuals? Should the church teach that sexual identity is negotiable, a matter of human choice so that, for example, the marriage of a transsexual should be celebrated in a church?

This last point has been helpfully discussed by Oliver O'Donovan, the current Regius Professor of Moral and Pastoral Theology at Oxford. O'Donovan insists that it is "important to the Christian understanding of marriage that it is contracted only between members of the opposite sex."[7] Marriage, he says, cannot be adequately described simply as a union between persons. Rather it "fulfills and so makes sense of" the fact that human beings "come into existence with a dimorphically differentiated sexuality, clearly ordered at the biological level toward heterosexual union as the human mode of procreation." He continues:

It is not possible to negotiate this fact about our common humanity; it can only be either welcomed or resented. Marriage, precisely by being organized around this fact, enables us to welcome it and to acknowledge it as a part of God's creational gift. . . . We learn through marriage to rejoice in the fact that humankind is sexually dimorphic and heterosexually procreative, because within marriage this non-negotiable biological datum enables us to form relationships of love between husband and wife, parent and child. . . . Other relationships . . . do not disclose the meaning of biological nature in this way.[8]

Biological nature is not "a problem to be overcome" and, unless disordered (in a hermaphrodite) is either male or female. (The *personality* characteristics of masculinity and femininity are distributed along a spectrum.)

O'Donovan argues that neither "sexual self-consciousness as a psychological phenomenon" nor "marriage as a social phenomenon" is independent of "the sexual identity conferred biologically."[9] Thus he insists that neither homosexual nor transsexual Christian marriage is a possibility, for in both cases the requisite biological difference is lacking. Human sexuality is not only genital, and it is not an artifact. Biological sexual differentiation is part of the order to the cosmos and an order that human medical technique must recognize, just as marriage should celebrate it.[10]

Even if it is exclusive about marriage, the church might bless "paramarital" relationships, but O'Donovan argues that a *policy* to do so would either suggest that sexual change is really possible or imply that homosexual or transsexual relationships were comparable to singleness. Such a policy would give pastoral flexibility, but "if a community declares that 'the truth shall make you free,' does it still have any scope to promote welfare by illusion?"[11]

This appeal to what is biologically natural is one that we have seen before in our discussion. I think O'Donovan is right to insist that marriage is a relationship intended to reflect sexual differentiation and to suggest caution about psychosocially indicated sex-change operations. On the other hand, his argument is most powerful when focusing on those humans who are clearly of one biological sex or the other. At least when biological hermaphroditism exists the "cosmic order" to which O'Donovan refers seems to have broken down. Probably there are human beings who cannot marry because of their biology—the church has made this affirmation about impotent males for centuries. But the hermaphroditism may not be total, and medical care to bring the body into line with identity should not be ruled out in such cases. The church's interest is in some clarity about marriage as such, and in pastoral sensitivity; the characteristic Anglican claim is that for marriage and human sexual fulfillment to be true they must conform to some objective facts.

That assertion becomes even more controversial in the discussion of homosexuality within Anglicanism. The communion has tried to come to terms with this issue for at least thirty years. Derrick Sherwin Bailey's *Homosexuality and the Western Christian Tradition*[12] was an early and remains a valuable treatment. His interpretation of the story of Sodom and Gomorrah, showing the problems with the old view of this story as reflecting a divine judgment on homosexuality, and his stress on the importance of a distinction between inversion (a fixed psychological orientation of love for the same sex) and perversion (acts that depart from one's nature, whatever it is) have set the terms for Anglican discussion of the issue. These are not characteristically focused on the Bible, and they recognize that a personal sexual orientation may be fate or destiny beyond the individual's control.

Naturally this does not mean that substantive consensus exists. On the one hand a personalist wing of the communion urges a celebration of homosexual community. Norman Pittenger writes that homosexual persons "are not deviant, but obviously they are different." The miracle of grace is that hetero- and homosexual persons can love.

> I should rejoice in the fact that there are people who love persons of their own sex, just as I rejoice in the fact that there are people who love persons of the other gender—it adds variety, color and spice to the common life, if only we will accept and help rather than reject and condemn.
>
> For it comes down to the theological conviction that God has worked in his creation to produce men and women of different kinds and interests, including sexual kinds and interests. Why should we not agree with this? I can think of no reason for failing to do so, except for inherited prejudice, dislike of what is not "our own thing" and failures in insight and charity.[13]

In contrast, more conservative writers favor toleration, but insist that homosexuality is not optimal or ideal. They insist that other factors besides the feelings of affection and love are relevant. Thus William Muehl:

> Let us end where we began. Homosexuality ought not to be treated as the manifestation of some special depravity whose practitioners should be driven from the church and harassed at law. But neither can it be defined as an appropriate expression of Christian love in interpersonal terms. The gay relationship is one form of sexual irresponsibility among many and no more reprehensible than most. Those involved in it have as much place in the pews as all the rest of us sinners. And as long as they recognize it as a

problem and are prepared to seek help in dealing with it, there should be no arbitrary limits placed upon their full participation as leaders in the Christian fellowship.

When gay people claim, however, that their way of life is a morally healthy one, insist upon their intention to affirm it publicly, and ask that it be consecrated in some way by the church, they put themselves in contempt of Christian conscience. Under such circumstances it is not only the right but the duty of other Christians to express grave misgivings about the seriousness of their faith and to challenge the wisdom of admitting homosexuals to positions of leadership in the churches.[14]

Why should one be grudging about equal status[15] when there is so much truth in what Pittenger says? The reason is the same as that which comes up in any discussion of a strictly personalist or situational morality: Human acts and commitments have consequences and significance beyond that which the actors may *choose* to invest in them. If I "destroy a village to save it" I cannot pretend I did not kill people, although the fact that my motives were good is certainly relevant in assessing my character. Just so, in considering sexual acts, the church must consider not only the motives of the human actors, but give some attention to the forms in which these motives become purposive activity. Then the hard issue arises. Is there reason to think there is something special about heterosexuality such that the church should keep it in a preferred place? I think so.

An interesting argument for this thesis has been advanced by Ruth Barnhouse, who follows Carl Jung's analysis of the sexual nature of persons. Women and men, she says, both include characteristically male and female (*anima* and *animus*) components in their personalities, but they integrate them in different ways. Persons who are fully mature will so integrate these components that their sexual loving focuses on the sexually other or different. This is a principle, a kind of "sacred order of the cosmos," "a general pattern to which we must conform." Sexuality is no more an end in itself than anything else; to deny this or act apart from the order is sin. Mature sexuality, in other words, symbolizes reunion. "[S]exuality itself is a symbol of wholeness, of the reconciliation of opposites, of the loving at-one-ment between God and creation . . . (and its true goal should not be seen) as *satisfaction* but *completeness*." Homosexuality, therefore, represents immaturity and "a symbolic confusion."[16]

Barnhouse opposes civil penalties for or discrimination against homosexual persons, but she insists that persons have some responsibility for their "immaturity." This includes "*all* failures of maturation" such as unwanted pregnancy and divorce. We have rightly ceased to treat these things in a judgmental way, but we should not forget that "every failure to take a possible maturational step has moral significance and falls under the rubric of original sin." Thus abortion, adultery and homosexuality should be dealt with "in the penitential mode, through compassion and forgiveness extended to those who are doing their best to take responsibility for their lives." Therefore "far from proclaiming their condition to be normal, homosexuals have the responsibility to minimize it so far as this lies within their power."[17]

There are several senses in which this more conservative view fits well with an Anglican ethic of fidelity: Epistemically it draws on a rich and culturally informed concept of natural or ideal human relations; liturgically it understands sexuality as imaging a reconciliation of estranged humankind and humans from each other; morally it maintains continuity with the core of traditional teaching, while purging it of its punitive aspect. The hard issue is its pastoral adequacy, for as Pittenger points out, there is a danger that the unconditional acceptance of all sinful persons will be selectively restricted so as to exclude those who are homosexual. And there can be no denying the moralistic note in Barnhouse's analysis of the human condition. Still, it is better to maintain a sense of an objective standard, gracefully applied across the board—to homosexual persons, adulterers and the self-righteous—than to risk an antinomian view that undercuts a radical challenge to growth.

Something of this balance was found in the 1980 Church of England Working Party Report on Homosexuality.[18] The Working Party argues that marriage as an institution is rooted in the sexual polarity of men and women. The institution must preserve both relations of love and reproduction. Thus marriage is rightly seen as involving a permanent commitment. And it provides the norm for sexual relations of all kinds. Persons capable of normal heterosexual relationships are wrong to engage in homosexual activities.

But for those to whom heterosexual community is impossible, homosexual expression may be appropriate "for as close an approximation as their condition permitted to what the heterosexual is able to enjoy in marriage." In sum, as Basil Mitchell, a member of the Working Party, put it:

> To insist upon an absolute prohibition, no matter how painful or abnormal the circumstances, would ... threaten the values underlying the principle itself or other principles to which the Christian is equally committed. To abandon the principle altogether, range all the cases on a single scale of lovingness, would be to ignore moral distinctions which are required by the nature of human life as God created it.[19]

Just as the church may tolerate polygamy but not celebrate polygamous marriage, so it may tolerate homosexual community when it is the only available cure for loneliness. But neither is equivalent to marriage.

The next aspects of marriage and sexuality that we should take up are associated with the procreation of new life. The marriage service itself now makes clear that children are not essential to the fulfillment of a marriage. The procreation of children is appropriate only "when it is God's will," whereas joy and companionship are presumed to be God's will in every marriage. But the procreation of children is clearly one theme in the marriage rite.[20] Moreover, the American prayer book has replaced the old rite for the "churching of women" after childbirth with a "Thanksgiving for the Birth or Adoption of a Child" which is aptly titled and involves rejoicing, an acknowledgment of parental responsibility (the rubrics stress making a will), and an affirmation that the child's fulfillment is found in relation to God. A central prayer is derived from this one of Jeremy Taylor:

> O Eternal God, who has promised to be a Father to a thousand generations of them that love and fear Thee; be pleased to bless this child who is newly come into a sad and most sinful world. O God, preserve his life, and give him the grace and sacrament of baptismal regeneration: do Thou receive him, and enable him to receive Thee, that he may have power to become the child of God; keep him from the spirits that walk at noon, and from the evil spirits of the night, from all charms and enchantments, from sudden death and violent accidents: give unto him a gracious heart and an excellent understanding, a ready and unloosed tongue, a healthful and a useful body, and a wise soul, that he may serve Thee, and advance Thy glory in this world, and may increase the number of Thy saints and servants in the kingdom of our Lord Jesus.[21]

So what are the issues? They arise because we have control over reproduction of a sort we never had before. This power creates the problem of how to use it. Here we can distinguish a series of sub-issues related to counseling, curtailing reproduction, use of new technologies for reproduction, nascent life and abortion.

COUNSELING

We should begin by discussing responsibilities of persons who are involved in decision-making about the beginning of life. This issue is increasingly important as the genetic basis for medical problems and techniques for prenatal diagnosis expand. John C. Fletcher, in his book *Coping with*

Genetic Disorders, establishes a helpful framework for genetic counseling. His focus is on the clergy, but we may take his description of ministry as "faithful companionship" as applicable to laity as well. Fletcher suggests that it is easy for Christian counselors or advisers to forget their own special role and to play, instead, the role of amateur physician, which leads the adviser into a quest for details and frantically chasing down the facts. To be sure, knowledge of the facts is important, but a companion's focus should be on other kinds of help needed by the client. To that end the companion should avoid being trapped as an advocate for one point of view or another. Rather he should start with honesty about his own feelings and help others recognize theirs. (I discussed Fletcher's views of truth-telling in chapter 2.)

Fletcher does not draw the conclusion that the adviser's role must be nondirective. Persons involved with a counselor may expect nondirection, as they imagine that the role of clergy parallels that of physicians—who, on this theory, merely sketch options. But a *moral* conclusion is not optional, as Fletcher rightly insists; it binds. Religious persons are bound by the rules and values of their traditions, as medical personnel are constrained by the rules of the institutions in which they work. Therefore, "if the clergy person acts in a way that demeans respect for the moral tradition, how can anyone else be expected to uphold it?"[22] Advisers cannot always be nondirective, but within the decision-making process Fletcher as a counselor must seek "a decision that makes moral sense and that fits into the ways and rules of the moral community whose values I must espouse." This is "must" in the sense of "must in order to preserve my self-respect"; integrity requires decisions that "I can square with my own need for self-respect and independence."[23]

Obviously this directive approach raises the question of what direction choices should move in. There is a limit on the generality with which that question can be answered, because it is not clear that setting eugenic goals is an appropriate activity of society as a whole. James Gustafson[24] outlines strategies the body politic might follow if it attempted to specify the goals of a positive or negative eugenics program—of breeding out defects or breeding in positive qualities. Theoretically we could appeal to generalizations about the healthy, or about the kinds of qualities that people in *any* society must have. We could defend our goals with reference to our individual traditions and beliefs. But none of these methods will persuade, as Gustafson goes on to note. Myopia, for example, is a serious genetic problem in some value systems but not in others, and many of the qualities we most want—such as compassion and a sense of justice—are not genetically determined. Thus as a practical matter society cannot set positive eugenic goals. That is an issue it should leave to its citizens as they work out their own life plans.

Precisely because society as a whole should stay out, it is important that persons have access to genetic information about themselves and/or their prospective children. They may misuse it, but possible misuse is not a good reason for failing to perform amniocentesis or censoring the results of genetic or prenatal testing. A community committed to truth must insist that people have a right to all unambiguous diagnostic results, whether they were explicitly requested or not. Failure to inform is not a legitimate way to bring about a eugenic goal, even if publicly legitimate goals could be stated.

What should parents do? Inform themselves, to be sure. (Fletcher will not celebrate a marriage in which the couple has not had genetic counseling.) But how much should eugenic worries control reproductive decisions? Our society manifests a physical perfectionism that, in my opinion, religious advice and counseling should oppose. Conceding that avoidance of the risk of serious defect is a fundamental responsibility, physical health is at most a necessary but not a sufficient condition for human excellence. Persons flourish in many walks of life, despite great physical handicap. Obviously, some handicaps preclude some kinds of excellence (there are few great blind golfers), but handicaps that rule out *all* kinds of human achievement are relatively few and rare.

Furthermore, excelling at everything is also rare. Virtues have a kind of specificity about them that precludes certain other kinds of virtues—it is hard to be resolute without being stubborn, and harder still to have this trait while one is "open to new possibilities" and flexible. How is one to judge which of these character traits and physical gifts will be needed or will be personal assets in the years ahead? Indeed, how can one predict the kinds of children that one's home will be able to nurture? History has not been encouraging on this point. I may want my daughter to be a doctor, but it is rare to be able to choose to be the kind of parent who will inspire that choice.

In fact, we may wonder whether the management of reproduction offered by our new powers is an unmixed blessing. Management and guidance are in themselves good things; the question is: Are there aspects of life that we should not try to guide, that are essentially destroyed if they are over-rationalized? Would it be good if we could decide about the sex, stature and intelligence of our children? Or is something lost in reproduction when the result is a carefully packaged product?

Think of the other end of life: Would it be good if we could all now know when, and of what causes, we will die? *That* we will die we should know and reflect on, as I have argued, but I am not sure the world would be better if death, the second major transition we experience, were totally controlled and predictable. Our ideal handling of death involves flexible responses whenever and however it may come. Preservation of that flexibility is itself a major human art and virtue, a treasure that would be lost in a society where death was "under control."

Generally, I am suggesting that loyal rationality about the beginning of life is *responsive* rather than *domineering*. The choice is not between reason and superstition, but between reason that is instrumental, subservient to certain humane purposes, and reason that is not. It is not a humane purpose to have *complete* control over one's own life, death or reproduction. At its root the natural lottery of human existence is not completely under our control. There is a natural facticity that breaks in with the birth of our children, and in our response to it our fundamental humanity is increased.

Bizarre as my point may be, I am eager not to be misunderstood. I do not mean that it is wrong to worry about one's family size or the genetic composition of one's children; I do not mean to imply that artificical insemination by donor (AID) or the conception of test-tube babies are wrong because a technician serves as a middleman. (Although I think we might ask ourselves why we would think it odd if someone preferred the test-tube method.) I mean to suggest that somewhere on this technological ladder (going up or down?) we move from an attitude that facilitates humility and loyalty in reproduction to one that refuses to live with the sterile, imperfect or unknown. And I think that to be a fateful and unfortunate moment.

Broadly speaking, there are two very different ways of responding to evil and imperfection. One way is activistic: The problem is taken on and straightforwardly solved. We have had great success with this approach in the past centuries. Progress has been astounding. Thus we have developed a sense of the ideal person: free, intelligent, dominant, confident. We expect the hero to continue to progress, and we expect to *be* the hero, more or less. And that's where the trouble comes in, because we find that we are really not very heroic, powerful or free. Our real lives are lives not of control, but of response; not of mastery, but of coping. We are not Prometheus.

Thus, we wonder if there is another way of responding to the suffering of a defective child, bad marriage or premature death. One often-misunderstood tradition in Anglicanism stresses the values of *acceptance*. As we have seen, the idea is that in consenting to be a person in the world one agrees to accept some of the bad along with the good. One cannot have the one without the other. The point is not that we should be afraid to alter our world *because* the new world we make might be inferior. (One of my colleagues has called this attitude the "Edsel syndrome.") The point is that a truly open self is vulnerable, likely to be harmed or affected by things beyond his or her control. When we overmanage, and overcontrol, we make it impossible for the world or others to give anything genuinely new to us.

Thus parents should avoid genetic risk when possible, but I do not think their goal-setting can plausibly go much beyond avoidance of certain clear and serious dangers, i.e., negative eugenics, and the counselor must help set the issue in perspective.

CURTAILING REPRODUCTION

We now have more subtle and precise ways of preventing conception than ever before. The only one of these that has been debated at length within Anglicanism is contraception; I will not take time here to trace the history of that discussion, but only note that its comparative recency and intensity suggest the depth of the tradition's commitment to the procreative side of marriage and a normative concept of the natural.[25] More pressing arguments today bear on the issue of sterilization.

A Church of England Working Party considered the question of sterilization in the 1960s. They argued that surgical cutting on the human body was justified in the past only when it was done for the sake of the whole body. This is the principle of totality: The part exists for the sake of the whole. If this principle were to be applied literally to questions of sterilization, the effect would be to justify only those sterilizing operations in which the purpose was removal of a diseased or damaged organ. Sterilization for eugenic or other contraceptive purposes would be forbidden and this is, in fact, the conservative Roman Catholic view. But the Church of England authors rejected it. "There is," they say, "a social dimension involved in all moral decision, even the most personal." Because we are social beings, the relevant "totality" for one of us to consider when thinking about sterilization should reflect "the fact that the patient's life is 'incorporate' with that of his spouse, his family, and the society or body politic of which he is a member." Therefore it is relevant to bear in mind the need for a community to regulate population, the need of a family adequately to provide for itself, and the need "of parents for some personal satisfaction in one another." Thus there are many possibly legitimate reasons for sterilization; the fact that the procedure is irrevocable should not preclude it on principle, for the church celebrates the irrevocableness of other decisions, e.g., marriage, and much surgery of other kinds is also irreversible.[26]

Consistent with this conclusion, I suggest that in deciding whether to be sterilized couples are fundamentally obliged to be loyal to each other. Loyalty requires that we be genuinely concerned for the good of another person and act accordingly. We ought to conduct ourselves so that the interests of our spouses are advanced. At the same time, being loyal does not mean signing a blank check for others. The old saying has it that a person is his own best friend, and loyalty requires taking care of one's own integrity.

Beyond this, the church's position does suggest that the burden of proof is on a choice for sterilization. To be sure, this is a burden that can be borne, for there may be many situations in which having children is a disservice to spouse, existing children or the wider community. But the choice to be sterilized requires asking the question: Is it the *least drastic* means available to attain an end that is *necessary*—either for physical or psychological health or for the sake of family or society?[27]

Given this framework, decisions for sterilization may be worthy of praise or blame, depending on the circumstances. Decisions to renounce parenthood through sterilization may be acts of courage and self-sacrifice —when parenthood would be desirable and when the obligation it might impose are displaced by higher and/or transcendent obligations. On the other hand, the choice of sterilization may reflect weaknesses of character. It may reveal an unwillingness to commit oneself, a failure of the courage that parenthood requires. Thus, it may stem from selfishness. Neither of these analyses of a decision for sterilization is necessarily true, nor are they necessarily mutually exclusive. The moral character lying behind a decision for sterilization is well hidden. In itself the decision is neither necessarily a product of vice nor virtue.

I would, therefore, only stipulate two necessary criteria for any sterilization decision based on loyalty:

1. A decision for sterilization forecloses not only possibilities for the self but for the husband or wife. Such decisions should not be made unilaterally, in violation of the bond of friendship with one's sexual partner, but collaboratively. Partner consent is essential.[28]

2. These decisions should not be made without sober thought about their possible effects on one's identity and self-image. One does a serious disservice to one's friends if one makes oneself a moral/personal cripple in pursuit of a good end that one lacks the strength to reach.

Can this reasoning lead to a justification of compulsory sterilization on eugenic grounds? Two factors, at least, force this issue to our attention. On the one hand, there may be some mentally retarded persons who could lead less cloistered lives if they were sterile, although their inability to consent would make the procedure involuntary. On the other hand, it is not obvious on the face of it that a person has an unlimited right to reproduce. Thus individual or social good might well be advanced by compulsory sterilization. Yet the Anglican communion will have to look long and hard to find circumstances in which compulsory sterilization is appropriate. We have to consider these facts:

a. Sterilization may be *perceived* by a patient as different from what it is. It may be seen as an attack on something much more central than it is, and the way the operation is perceived is relevant to what is done to the patient as a person. Compulsory sterilization is not just altering a physiological mechanism, but is an assault on a self.

b. The past history of eugenic-sterilization laws in the United States is not encouraging. Generally these suggest the finitude of our knowledge. Suppose we were to accept compulsory sterilization. Would we be able to agree on criteria for selection of patients? Are those criteria to concern only the health of the patient or long-range eugenic goals? Shall they include a referent to socioeconomic factors? These questions are unanswered and may be unanswerable.

For reasons like these the Church of England Working Party rejected the compulsory sterilization of retarded but noninstitutionalized persons, not only because the principle involved was wrong but because sterilization offered the patient only "incomplete protection" from sexual mistakes or exploitation and because the "less drastic remedy" of "integration . . . into the life of the community, providing . . . such support and protection as they need in the conduct of their lives" should be made available.[29]

Compulsory sterilization is wrong, then, because it involves serious risks to the person of the patient, because it is of dubious effect and necessity, and because it is unclear that we can formulate criteria for its fair use.

This said, I should go on to add that I would not preclude an informing and educating function by health professionals and public officials. I hold no brief for the view that directive counseling is tantamount to coercion. Vigorous persuasion may be in order if, in fact, we are really to play fair with some patients. So long as all sides of the picture are presented I am untroubled by this strategy, for I find it highly preferable to the increasingly widespread practice of "eugenic" abortion.

NEW TECHNOLOGIES FOR REPRODUCTION

Sterility, an objective for some, is a problem for others. Medical science now has some remarkable ways of overcoming sterility. One is artificial insemination, using semen from husband (AIH) or donor (AID). Another is in vitro fertilization in which an egg cell is fertilized outside the body and then reimplanted in the womb of the donor or another woman. Obviously these possibilities can be combined in various ways so that several different kinds of degrees of separation between genetic, biologically nurturant and social parenthood are possible. Important, if misleading, phrases in the current discussion are "test-tube babies" and "surrogate mothering."

The 1982 General Convention of the Episcopal Church received a report from its Standing Commission on Human Affairs and Health that addressed these issues as well as birth control and abortion. The commission supported use of male surrogates (AID) but not female (surrogate mothers) because of the psychological risks to and/or exploitation of the surrogate childbearer. They reject use of surrogating to provide a child for single parents as "the mainstream of American narcissism and self-indulgence,"[30] but they were careful not to condemn the technique of in vitro fertilization as such. The convention as a whole urged provision of genetic counseling, favored pre-natal diagnosis and in vitro fertilization when used as a technique to enable conception by a childless couple, but was cautious about surrogate parent-ing and the sale of human semen.[31]

Some of the issues raised by these technologies concern the status of and our responsibilities to the conceptus—zygote, embryo, fetus and child— that may result from the procedures. I want to hold those issues in abey-ance for a moment, and ask whether these technologies present problems even if duties to the engendered being should not figure into our reckoning at all. Two complexes of issues come to mind. They do not lead to a neces-sary social policy conclusion, but they suggest that the issues are serious and they point in a direction.

The first complex of issues surrounds the question of whether it is morally right to separate the human community of reproduction from the commu-nity of sexual love. Is it important that the person with whom one makes a baby be the same as the person with whom one makes love? These two forms of community are *not* separated when a married couple uses in vitro fertilization with their own gametes, but they would be separated if one were to use donor eggs, or host mothers who would carry children for women unable or unwilling to be pregnant. Separation also happens with AID; even the adoption of children always involves a separation of biological and social parenting. (Beautiful as adoption is, would we not reject the *intentional* conception of children whom one intended to put up for adoption?) The new technologies of reproduction will increasingly be used when natural reproduction is problematical. But consider:

First, selfhood is always historical. We develop a concept of ourselves and a sense of identity in relationship to persons around us. Part of this development has to do with knowing what our relationship is to others. In the "normal" case one understands this very well. My identity is that of the child of a specific set of parents and the grandchild of four grandparents. I think of myself as embodied, and embodied with physical material that is specific; it comes from those roots with all their twists, turns and resiliences. I know the characteristic vices (and perhaps a few virtues); I know the common causes of death; I know of myopia and bad teeth and several hundred other things too trivial and uninteresting to mention.

But they are not uninteresting *to me*, for they are constitutive of who I am. The more I know my roots, the more I know myself. Part of the sociopathology of our time is that through divorce, social mobility and many other cultural changes we are increasingly cut off from those roots, for we define ourselves in relationship to our parents, and that includes a self-definition in relation to their physical being.

When we separate biological origins from family community we complicate this matter still further. The child growing up in such a situation perceives a gap between the roots of self and the roots of body; the child's world is fractured in some ways that others' worlds are not. This is not to say that other fractures are trivial—they may be far worse—or to say that the child's particular tension is of unusually great importance. It is only to say that it is a problem, that a child conceived with donor gametes asks "Who am I?" in ways that other persons do not.

Second, we should examine the intentionality that underlies chosen reproduction with a nonlover. Why would one feel that reproduction is so important that this step must be taken? To make my bitter point let me focus on the intentionality of the partner whose gametes are plentiful and available—the one who is fertile. I mean the woman in an AID situation or the man in the case of a contemplated egg donation. This fertile partner is purchasing "authentic" (i.e., genetic) parenthood for himself or herself when that possibility is closed to the spouse. That a loving *sterile* spouse will go along with this course I do not mean to deny or condemn, but I want to raise the question of why the fertile partner insists on having this good *alone*. If the couple wants the social experience of parenting, they can have it in another wonderful way, i.e., through adoption.

Conceding that *ceteris paribus* it is more gratifying to conceive one's own children than adopt them, the fertile partner faces a choice between reproduction in which my spouse and I are equal partners—partners in what we do not have as well as in what we have—or reproduction in which I have a full kind of gratification and my spouse does not. Consider an analogy: Suppose someone could choose between great riches for himself and a smaller income, equally divided and accessible to self and spouse. Which ought to be chosen? The latter option of sharing is the more loyal choice.

Put bluntly, I am suggesting that the hubris that is often a major motivation in human reproduction is especially likely to be related to reproduction using the new technologies, in particular when donor gametes are at issue. The problem is especially pronounced when we think of the still remote possibility of cloning human beings. In the case of cloning one maneuvers to avoid the chance of watering down an assumedly ideal genotype; in the case of gamete donation one is unwilling or unable to surrender one's private hopes to the ambiguities of a joint project: marriage. In both cases the pride may be concealed by what C. D. Broad once called self-referential altruism, a self-deception that describes and defends the actions chosen in self-sacrificial terms. But in both cases a striking kind of self-assertion remains.

Thus I think the church's conception of selfhood as embodied and its notion of marriage as a deep and avowed commitment of the self suggest that it should, at least, say the burden of proof is on someone who chooses surrogating, and that flat-out opposition, even to AID, should be seriously considered.[32]

NASCENT LIFE

Once conception occurs, the issue changes. Or does it? The hard question is just how much to count the early products of conception. I will suggest that it is impossible to give an adequate *general* answer to that question, but I shall also contend that we know enough to handle the issues before us.

It is convenient to begin at the very start of gestation, for one issue that is inevitably raised by the new reproductive technologies concerns the status of the early human embryo. This may seem to be an overly refined issue. Some readers of this book have washed fertilized human ova down the drain with less compunction than they would have over the killing of a rat, and some are women who have "miscarried" many very early embryos.

They have not mourned, or even known of, these events. Somehow it seems slightly overscrupulous, lacking in perspective, to be worried about the fate of these tiny organisms, similar to us only in chromosomal composition. If we could be clear in our minds that the early embryo is trivial, some of the issues raised by in vitro fertilization would be immensely simplified.

Clarity on this point is especially important for two reasons. First, only a small fraction of human embryos conceived by in vitro fertilization will go to term. That is, there is considerable risk of loss of life to the embryo. Second, these embryos are brought into their dangerous situation intentionally. The circumstances are very different from those in many abortions where the pregnancy "problem" that has to be "solved" is an accident. The existence of the fertilized human ovum is certainly someone's responsibility. These facts are unimportant if the embryo is unimportant, but as it increases in importance these factors become proportionately more important. We cannot conclusively resolve the matter, but we want as much clarity as we can get. Let us examine the options:

1. Should the embryo be understood to be a person with the same kinds of rights that the rest of us have? "Conceptionalists"[33] argue that they are persons, but their contentions seem to confront serious difficulties. The most fundamental of these problems cluster around our conviction that personhood is a moral and psychological as well as, or instead of, a strictly biological matter. We can get at this in various ways, I suppose. One would involve a kind of "thought experiment." Beginning with our rudimentary sense that personhood usually involves a soul and a body, we can ask ourselves which of those two "parts" is most fundamental. Which is more personlike: a robot that has mental states and a will like ours, or a comatose human body? Granting that neither is completely impersonal, I suggest that the robot comes closer.

We can imagine persons with very extensive prosthetic devices substituted for their limbs and organs, but we cannot imagine beings as persons who completely lack the capacity for moral action. That is, it does not make sense to speak of persons when we cannot speak of moral agency. If the entity in question cannot be praised or blamed for his or her actions, then the entity is not a person. He or she does not have rights in the same sense of that word as you and I do. Because the embryo is not a person the nonmoral or natural evil involved in the embryo's death is less serious than the nonmoral or natural evil that would be involved in mine. Duties we may have to it have a different basis or grounding than the duties we have to one another. No one seriously proposes that embryos should be baptized.

2. The extreme alternative to the conceptionalist view is the claim that

embryos have no special moral status at all. They are simply what one of my colleagues once called "biological material" to be put to those uses that will be most beneficial to the rest of us. This view is attractive in its logical consistency, but it is also not without its problems. For one thing, it ignores the fact of potentiality. I do not mean to claim too much for this argument, as I think that it is often misused, but I do want to note that it is very hard to find clear lines that can be drawn in the human developmental process after conception. The fertilized ovum is an organism that naturally will develop into a human being. This development may be impeded by other natural forces and/or by persons, but it does seem to distinguish the human embryo from sperm, eggs or fertilized rat ova. And this distinction is strictly on the biological level. Thus it would seem fairer to put the burden of proof on a denial of special status than on arguments designed to establish that status.

Related to this point, it is relevant to observe that the holders of the "biological-material" view have trouble explaining why we ought to ascribe special status to late fetuses, newborn babies or even preschool children, some beings we might and others we do baptize. Attempts to find a cutoff point that focuses on the use of language, on brain waves, or on some sort of self-concept have proven to be notoriously ambiguous.

I have already conceded that embryos are not persons in the fullest sense of that term, but I have not denied either that they are potential persons or that they may have some kind of significance different from that which we assign to persons. A denial of any preferred moral or ontological status to the embryo is a much stronger claim than a denial of personal status to the same entity. And making the stronger negative claim gets one into very serious difficulty for stages of human development between embryo and adult human being. One has, so to speak, reduced one's moral options to a stark either/or: either personal dignity and rights or nothing. Once this option is accepted, requirements of logical consistency push one to the conclusion that many beings once thought to be special (e.g., babies) are not preferable to chimpanzees. If this is a mistake, it may mean that other options should be considered.

3. The major one of these options that I want to discuss is the idea that early human concepti are special and therefore are to be treated with respect. They are not persons, but they bear a kind of "image of personhood"; they are resources for the future enrichment of our community of persons.

I should like to argue for this idea in a couple of ways and to suggest something of what it might imply. The arguments for it begin, I think, with a conviction of the inadequacy of the alternatives, which I have already attempted to show. But we can go on to note that a denial of this claim says something about the overall worldview or perspective of the denier. If we deny it, we are denying either or both (a) the importance of potentiality and a concomitant requirement to nurture, or (b) the status of the human physical body in personal life.

It is possible to deny that things grow and that human persons can influence their growth for good or ill, but this denial seems to have striking implications for our philosophy of the world and for the role of human agency in that world. Quite the contrary, most of us understand that seeds will grow to flowers and that the quality and quantity of flowers grown is to a significant extent a function of human nurturing. That is, we accept the idea that a flower seed has a kind of special status because of its relationship to the mature plant, and we think it sensible to praise or blame human agents who alter the plant's growth patterns. We neither believe in the spontaneous creation of daisies nor in the irrelevance of watering. To be consistent, we ought to make similar affirmations about germinal persons and our obligations to them.

Furthermore, consistent denials of the special significance of the embryo seem to imply that there is nothing especially sacred about human "biological material" or, to put it baldly, the human body. Such a claim contravenes not only Anglican celebration of the creation but the very deep intuitions of most of us. For, at the risk of being gross, we should notice that one very fundamental repugnance we share is an aversion to cannibalism. Yet cannibalism would—and sometimes does—make infinite sense. We reject it, I submit, not because of pacifistic rejections of killing or because of respect for persons. Both those principles can be bypassed. We reject cannibalism because we think or feel that there is something special about human tissue as such.[34] We reckon as perverse communities that do not share this valuation.

Thus our general view of the world and our commitment to the body require us to put the early products of human conception into some kind of special moral category. What are the implications of this? I am feeling my way here, but I offer two suggestions.

One component in our treatment of persons is the intentionality that we bring to bear on them. We expect persons to have a just, loving or fair bearing toward one another. It seems appropriate to give the same to the embryo. Things should not be done that are not potentially to its benefit. To create it in vitro, to implant or try to bring about its implantation—those are actions for its benefit (that might also be learned from). Treatment that offers it no hope of benefit should be ruled out. No nontherapeutic experimentation.

Second, at a minimum we assume that loyalty to persons means looking out for their bodies as best we can. We might say, "Not only hasn't he educated his children, he hasn't even given them coats for their backs." Thus we assume responsibilities for the protection of persons. Analogously, we ought to protect the embryo as far as possible and should minimize risk to it. The safest possible means of fertilization and gestation should be chosen.

This is a very fuzzy category, of course, for no human life or pregnancy is devoid of risk. The embryo in vitro need not be kept safer than her brother in vivo. But this caveat does not destroy the overall point: Increase of risk counts against the morality of a technique of conception, however laudable the ultimate goods to be brought about.

If any of this argument is plausible, we must go on to say that the developing embryo or fetus becomes more personlike and important with the passage of time. Necessarily there is some ambiguity and uncertainty about this. Gordon Dunstan writes that "as we do not know at what precise point in the five million years the anthropoid ape became man, so we do not know at what point in the nine months in the womb the conceptus becomes 'human' (i.e., a person)." Because personhood is an attributed status, he continues, it is "an imposition from the human cultural tradition upon the genetic inheritance"; the necessary moral protections are not self-evident but have to be worked out.[35] Since human nature in God's image is relational, Dunstan inclines to locate the crucial point when "maternal presence" awakens the fetus's "potential for human response" and the mother's awareness of her pregnancy initiates "the beginning of maternal response." Dunstan suggests these changes may correlate with development of the conceptus's cerebral cortex and occur within the first six weeks.[36]

But maternal consciousness may occur much later, at "quickening," when fetal movement is felt. Thus it is probably better to acknowledge that "the concept of a human being is to some extent indeterminate" so that its use to ascribe rights to fetuses is problematical; to insist that fetal development makes a difference, so that late abortions are more weighty matters than early ones; and to affirm that nascent life always counts for something. Although we cannot univocally establish the status of the fetus, we can say that late ones are more personlike than early ones, and when we turn to the abortion question itself we can affirm fetal inviolability as a first principle that may, for weighty reasons, sometimes be compromised.[37]

ABORTION[38]

How should Christian parents decide when faced with a pregnancy that is problematical because of known fetal defect or for some other reason?

Is a decision for abortion congruent with the basic affirmations of Christian conscience as Anglicans know it? Answers to this question range all the way from Joseph Fletcher's approval of any freely chosen abortion decision to the total exclusion of this particular possibility. These extremes seem to me to distort the complex ingredients in the Anglican tradition and experience as well as to oversimplify the practical problem. Various lines of analysis must be made and somehow woven together, beginning with something like the following strands:

1. The fundamental Christian affirmation is that through Jesus Christ human beings are related to the greatest power and the most profound truth that are to be found. This power and truth is called God. Within Anglicanism Christian conscience is always relational. Persons do not, ultimately, live by themselves: They live, according to Christian confession, with God through Christ.

The first relevant implication of this fact for reasoning about abortion is that it suggests that God, rather than persons, is sovereign over the world. This idea is captured in the creation stories, in the recurrent metaphor of the "kingdom" of God—so central in ancient Israel and the proclamation of Jesus—and of course in the Lord's Prayer—"Thy kingdom come. . . ." Probably I do not need to go on. The point to stress at this stage is the negative one: God's sovereignty implies the less-than-ultimate sovereignty of human persons. We are children of God, but we are not God. Thus we should not make absolutes of our fears, hopes or purposes.

The implication for reasoning about abortion is that disruption of established and gratifying life-patterns, forced changes of plans, the necessity completely to rethink and rework personal and family expectations—all these, and many more, challenges that a prospective child implies are not really challenges to something unquestionably right. If God is sovereign, people must learn to sit loose to comfortable habits and dreams. The necessity to rethink a present set of values, and the future, should come as no surprise to the Christian. Thus one ingredient in the conscientious consideration of abortion should be a willingness to put one's prior plans and values at least temporarily into the realm of the provisional. The Christian does not pray, "*my* kingdom come."

On the other hand, Christians claim that the fundamental use God has made of his sovereignty has been to involve himself with, to relate himself to, the world. The same creation stories that imply God's transcendence suggest the goodness of nature as his product. And human nature, in particular, takes on value from adopted sonship: Thus persons are made "in the image of God" with dominion over the creation; the Christian claim is that God disclosed himself in a person; indeed a vigorous recent critique of traditional Western Christianity is that it is excessively "anthropocentric." Anglicanism confesses that because of God's special relation to human persons, human life is sanctified. Thus Anglicans cannot argue that fetuses cease to make claims because they are young, dependent, not fully developed or invisible.

2. Life before God has certain definite characteristics, as I have suggested throughout this book. There are some things that are given; three of them of some relevance here.

a. To begin with, our individual lives are involved in relationships with several other human beings. We cannot help but be bound to or concerned with more than one other person. Thus, supposing us to have obligations to others, these obligations are diverse and may well conflict. There is always more than one person, more than one relationship, to be taken into account. Consequently, reasoning about a possible abortion cannot bracket off consequences for spouse, siblings or fellow workers, any more than it can discount a sense of obligation to the fetus. Effects on all others, and on the self, are relevant to any abortion decision.

b. Furthermore, the natural world in which we live has characteristics that must be related to this decision. Sexuality is reproductive: The "best" sex leads beyond itself to personal novelty and growth, and nothing is more novel than a human child. Indeed, "there is an inherent connection between a responsible—it is not too much to say reverential—attitude to sexual relationships and reverence for life." Persons are "devalued equally in loose and irresponsible attitudes to sexual relationships and in a light regard for unborn and infant life."[39]

Beyond these psychological claims the basic biological point remains that human sexual acts of love may have procreative consequences undesired by lovers. Sometimes those are consequences for which couples are responsible. Responsibility for pregnancy resulting from an ill-fitting diaphragm is different from responsibility for pregnancy caused by failure to take any contraceptive precautions. An attempt to deny responsibility for the latter pregnancy, on the basis of an appeal to desires or "intentions," only shows an inability accurately to perceive the nature of the world in which we live.

Consequently, in reasoning about abortion the circumstances of conception are of considerable relevance. Many males, it sometimes seems, regard all pregnancies as occurrences "caused" by women, as the result of female *actions*. Women, in contrast, often think of pregnancy as something that *happens to* them. Later I will stress the truth in the second (female) interpretation. For now, I merely mean to note that there are some times when the "male" view is correct—when unwanted pregnancy is a woman's, and/

or her lover's, responsibility. Insofar as someone is responsible for the pregnancy, a justification of abortion becomes more problematical.

c. Finally, we should note the very general implication of individual human finitude of knowledge and discernment. There is always the possibility that one's perceptions are wrong, that one can learn from the individual and collective judgments of others. Moreover, we face a constant tendency toward self-deception. As a result the standards of society become of considerable relevance. Such conventions may, of course, be perverse. Legalization of abortion does not make it right. But the existence of social prohibitions, regulations and/or permissions are morally relevant facts.

3. Christians understand themselves to have an ideal character in their life before God. I have repeated that this is best described as a life of loyalty, of passion for God and compassion for others. The New Testament portraits of Jesus are the basis for the sketch of this ideal. They show a man faithful to the needs of his fellows. The needs of the weak and helpless are stressed.

Given all we have said, is a life of fidelity compatible with a decision for abortion? The major justification for taking life in Christian tradition has been protection. Human life as the highest value under God could be destroyed only to protect other human life. Defective fetuses may threaten lives and so can be reasoned about in this way. Then the hard questions arise—what is the exact extent and kind of the harms done to others by the fetus's life? Are the psychological strain, social and economic dislocation equivalent to the price an aborted fetus will pay? Is the fact that the fetus is caught in this situation anyone's responsibility? Are there alternatives that would allow the fetus to live, yet save the endangered other persons? In conscience it may be that these questions can be answered in a way that abortion is justified, but that justification will not be the usual result.

Further, however, it may be that some fetuses have a need to die that finite persons in fidelity should respect or even work to meet. The fact that a faithful decision to abort because of Down's syndrome will be rare, should not blind one to the possibility that a life may be very likely to be nasty, brutish and short. Antenatal diagnosis of Tay-Sachs disease, Lesch-Nyhan syndrome, or anencephaly would—if certain—raise this possibility. However, even in these cases, it is essential to focus on the certain sufferings of the expected child and to distinguish these from statistical possibilities and suffering expected by the parents. For the former may not materialize and the latter shows an unfortunate willingness to trade off against the interests of the conceptus. Decision-makers should focus on the needs and prospects of the specific defective fetus. Comparisons with the prospects of "healthy" fetuses should be ruled out. Is the disorder so severe that the only good we can bring to the fetus is a ministry and fidelity to the fetus's death? If so, we should act accordingly.

In sum, Anglican conscience will tend to be conservative about the decision to abort. Arguments from protection of others and from fidelity to the fetus are both admissible on principle, but neither will often lead to the conclusion that a decision for abortion is compatible with Christian life.

4. This conclusion leaves open the question of who should decide whether the threat is sufficiently severe, or the fetal prognosis sufficiently bleak, to justify abortion. Judgment is called for, but whose shall it be? I think that within certain limits it should be the pregnant woman's judgment, for the following reasons.

Earlier in this book I suggested that loyalty requires equal concern for various parties in a conflict situation. *Ceteris paribus*, people have equal needs to exist, to act and to choose for themselves. We understand ourselves to be obliged to act to feed, clothe, medicate and educate. On the other hand, our commitment to equality means that we cannot provide any one individual, of any age, with everything he or she may need. Our responsibilities to other individuals must be limited by the fact that we must consider the needs of several people. There are times when we must say, in effect, "Although she needs it, I (we) cannot give it."

What then does loyalty require of women to the fetuses they carry? It is hard for me to see how these obligations can be seen as an exception to the general rule on limited liability. Pregnant women have other legitimate loyalties besides those to fetuses in utero, so duties to the conceptus are not absolute. Professor Judith Thomson made a similar point in a justly well-known essay.[40] She creates the hypothetical situation of a person who awakens to discover that all his vital systems have been connected to those of the world's greatest violinist. The violinist is suffering from a serious disease and can only survive the next nine months if his "host" remains in bed and connected to him. Could one say the host is "obliged" to spend the next months so constrained? Professor Thomson argues that one cannot. Such a self-sacrificial decision would be noble, but it cannot be *required* of anyone, especially someone with other pressing loyalties.

Attacks that I have heard on this argument from analogy usually stress the disanalogy of cause. The critics argue that waking up pregnant is not a surprise like that experienced by the person with the violinist hookup. People become pregnant because they made love, and lovemaking is procreative.

Thus, so the criticism seems to run, women are always responsible for being pregnant.

My partial sympathy for this point of view has, I hope, already come out, but it is important to observe that this objection glosses over the frequent occurrence of *responsible accidental* pregnancy. Pregnancy following rape is the obvious, but by no means the only, case. Generally, many pregnancies in stable relationships following contraceptive failure must be described as responsibly accidental. In such cases it is Draconian to refer to the pregnancy as something *caused* by the woman. Rather, as most women perceive, those pregnancies are things that *happen to* women. In this sense the wide availability of effective contraceptives is a very significant moral fact; if they did not exist, it would be impossible to intend nonprocreative lovemaking. Since contraceptives are available, however, we must see that although not every unwanted pregnancy is "responsibly accidental," some are.

The implication, of course, is that women cannot be understood to be unconditionally obliged to carry "accidental" pregnancies, with or without fetal defect, to term. There is a legitimate space for individual choice in the matter.

Abortions that follow pregnancies for which couples are responsible (nonaccidental) are, however, not justified by this line of reasoning. If a couple either meant to conceive or failed to take reasonable contraceptive precautions, they cannot then claim that the pregnancy or the perilous situation of the fetus are facts for which they have no responsibility. Sissela Bok has considered the distinction involved with some vigor. She concedes that "there are many cases where these distinctions cannot be so clearly made. It may be difficult to know whether there was an intention to have a baby or to risk becoming pregnant.[41] Yet, she rightly suggests, some difficult problems of line-drawing do not invalidate the importance of the distinction at issue.

In fact, the only problem with Professor Bok's discussion involves her reluctance to press the distinction involved as far as it will go. Unfortunately, she does not explicitly say that some *unwanted* pregnancies are, nevertheless, pregnancies for which lovers are responsible. Thus she implies that absence of the *desire* to have a child is the crucial moral fact. According to Professor Bok, omission of contraceptive measures is not immoral but "insensitive" when abortion is used as a check.

The degree of responsibility for conception affects the morality of an abortion decision. Bok suggests three different degrees of responsibility through use of an analogy with death by drowning. We can schematize them as follows:

1. X drowns, and a passer-by, Y, does not attempt to save him.	1. The abortion of a fetus conceived against a woman's wishes.
2. X drowns after swimming where/when Y assured him it was safe.	2. The abortion of a fetus conceived despite certainty of being "protected against pregnancy."
3. X drowns after Y pushes him into the water.	3. The abortion of an intentionally conceived pregnancy.

The basic point is that responsibility (on the part of Y or the pregnant woman) for death in the third situation is much greater than in the first. My difficulty is that a wide range of cases fall under the second situation, so that the category should be subdivided as follows:

2a. X drowns after swimming on the advice of a well-informed and reasonable friend, Y.	2a. The abortion of a fetus conceived despite reasonable contraceptive precautions.
2b. X drowns when a friend (Y) urges him to water ski at night immediately after a party.	2b. The abortion of a fetus conceived when no or inadequate contraceptive precautions are taken.

The friend of the drowned person (Y) and the parents of the fetus have, I suggest responsibilities in 2b that their counterparts do not have in 2a. Although they did not consciously plan for (or cause) a death to occur (and thus differ from case 3), they do have responsibility for the situation in virtue of their negligence and prior actions. If this is so, then failure to use adequate contraceptives is not "insensitive" but, like drunken driving, it is immoral. In neither case should an appeal to wishes absolve from moral responsibility.

The number of responsible accidental pregnancies (1, 2a), then, is not as great as might be supposed. Certainly it is smaller than the number of "unwanted" pregnancies, but it nevertheless exists. With this thought in mind, we ask again who is to decide if a particular pregnancy is one that should be terminated, a question that in part involves the issue of whether a given pregnancy is one for which people are responsible—or an accident that occurred. One logical possibility is decision by a public board that would inquire into the circumstances of conception as well as a range of other matters, but such agencies have proven themselves inconsistent, arbitrary and discriminatory.[42] Others suggest that fathers should have a veto power, forgetting that many fathers take no responsibility for their partners or their children. Thus the only plausible final decision-maker is the pregnant woman herself, who may, of course, make a moral mistake. She is not an ideal decision-maker, but all other possibilities are worse.

This fact of maternal sovereignty, however, is no justification for isolated decision-making or desertion. In discussing other decisions for death I stressed the importance of consultation and discussion. This factor was stressed in the fine Church of England pamphlet, *Abortion: An Ethical Discussion*, whose argument I have largely followed. There are two differences: The authors of *Abortion* do not allow that fetal defect can be an independent justification for abortion. It is, they say, only relevant insofar as fetal defect may contribute to a threat to the mother's life. Even here the disagreement may not be as great as first appears, for my argument for maternal discretion does not establish a right to kill a viable fetus —i.e., one that others could save. There is a distinction between choosing to disengage oneself and choosing death for another. Pregnant women have jurisdiction over the first but not the second choice. Let me explain.

Late fetuses are not only like persons in certain significant respects, they are or soon will be *viable*, i.e., savable by someone besides the mother. Abortion techniques like saline injection are ways of doing something besides liberating the mother. They are ways of ensuring that no one else will save, nurture and care for the fetus. Except in the very rarest instance, therefore, they are immoral. This is a consideration that should regulate medical policy and perhaps our laws.

Abortions before viability, in contrast, do not create quite the same problem for society, since they do not involve the community as a whole in destroying a life it can save. The only way a public group could ensure the safety of nonviable fetuses is by denying to women responsibilities for choice that, I contend, they should have. It is not exactly that society must condone and /or approve of all early abortions, any more than we condone thousands of daily deaths from automobile accidents. Rather, our recognition of maternal responsibility means that society must tolerate a certain amount of unjustified sacrifice of fetal life.

Moreover, there may be late fetuses for whom the life prospects are so bleak that they are better off dead, but a decision for the death of a viable fetus should be made solely with reference to its prospects; it is indistinguishable from the parallel choices about defective newborns that I discussed in chapter 5. Thus morally legitimate decisions for death will be few. While I depart from the authors of *Abortion* in my argument for female responsibility, I do not disagree with their justifications for killing.

Thus the main difference between my view and that of *Abortion* has to do with the locus of decision-making responsibility. The authors of *Abortion* insist that it should reside in the community generally, in a medically focused process, rather than being a matter of maternal right. Although it seemed to agree with this, the abortion-law reform passed by Parliament in the 1960s included several independent indications (rape, fetal defect, threat to mother) rather than simply a broadly defined maternal indication. At least one author of *Abortion* feels that the history of abortion-law reform and practice in Britain has been disastrous, "compromising the Church of England with an enactment to which its Bishops, with one exception, were in principle opposed."[43] As a result the number of abortions has risen far beyond what is reasonable. "One longstanding convention is being swept away. Those who regret its passing have a clear moral duty. It is to strive with concerted might to create conditions for its return—or for its replacement with something better."[44]

In my view, however, the best means to this end is not to take decision-making power from women. It is rather to require counseling before and after abortions,[45] to encourage discussions of sexual morality in church and school—discussions focusing on responsibility and the requirements of relationships, rather than on technique—and to insist on social supports for the parents of handicapped or any "unwanted" children—a point Dunstan himself makes with characteristic force.

Thus, in summary, our loyalties require the honoring of a female prerogative to terminate pregnancy. Before viability this is equivalent to a right to decide to destroy the fetus; after viability it is not. Anglicanism leads parents to think in terms of responsibility—for other persons, for nascent life, for the limitations of their preconceptions and projects, for cowardice and self-deception. These considerations may lead to a choice for abortion, but only when the choice is an act of fidelity. Loyalty, not liberty, is the fundamental concern.

Christmas and Good Friday epitomize moments of beginning and ending within Anglicanism. Perhaps no medical procedure draws them into closer juxtaposition than abortion, for none better shows the possibilities and agonies of our age. The church should not fear to insist on the stakes in these, as in all, medical decisions. But its final words should be of Easter and reconciliation. The community must live with ambivalence and disagreement within it. Broken, it must find a way to come together. Agreement and unanimity are not to be expected, but compassion and loyalty are essential to communion among the children of God.

Notes

Preface

1. John Booty's essay will appear in *Caring and Curing: Health and Medicine in the Western Religious Traditions*, ed. Darrel Amundsen and Ronald Numbers (New York: Macmillan, forthcoming).

Chapter 1/Anglicanism

1. Anthony Shaw, "Dilemmas of Informed Consent in Children," *New England Journal of Medicine* 289 (Oct. 25, 1973): 886.
2. Janelle Goetcheus, *A Physician Cries Out: The Non-System of Health Care for the Urban Poor*, Shalom Paper No. 9 (Washington, D.C.: Churches' Center for Theology and Public Policy, 1980), pp. 3–4.
3. David Jenkins, *The Glory of Man* (New York: Charles Scribner's Sons, 1967), pp. 55–59.
4. Ibid., p. 89.
5. Ibid., p. 106.
6. George MacDonald, quoted in C. S. Lewis, *The Problem of Pain* (New York: Macmillan and Co., 1962).
7. Robert A. Lambourne, *Community, Church and Healing* (London: Darton, Longman and Todd, 1963), pp. 71ff.
8. Cicely Saunders, "Dimensions of Death" in M. A. H. Melinsky (ed.), *Religion and Medicine: A Discussion*, 2 vols. (London: SCM Press, 1970), 1:116. Cf. Herbert Waddams, *A New Introduction to Moral Theology* (New York: The Seabury Press, 1965), p. 200: "Christian teaching does not maintain that one should suffer because it is good for the character, as it is sometimes represented. It does teach that suffering cannot be escaped in this world, and that it can be entered into and made into moral and spiritual victory, and that there are some depths and heights of personal development which can be reached in no other way than through suffering."
9. Richard Hooker, *Laws of Ecclesiastical Polity*, Sixth Edition (Oxford: Keble, 1874), V.60.2.
10. Ibid., V.67.5.
11. Ibid., V.67.2.
12. Ibid., V.68.5.

13. Ibid., V.56.1.
14. Ibid., V.56.6.
15. Ibid., V.56.9.
16. Ibid., V.54.5.
17. J. F. D. Maurice, *The Kingdom of Christ* (London: SCM Press, 1958), Vol. I, p. 228.
18. Ibid., pp. 242f.
19. Kenneth Kirk, *Conscience and Its Problems* (London: Longmans, Green and Co., 1927), p. 101.
20. Hooker, *Laws*, I.3.5.
21. Ibid., I.10.12.
22. Robert Sanderson, Sermon IV, *Sermons ad Populum Works*, Vol. III, pp. 101ff. Quoted in Thomas Wood, *English Casuistical Divinity During the Seventeenth Century* (London: SPCK, 1952), pp. 58f.
23. Everett C. Hughes, *Cycles and Turning Points*, A Faculty Paper by the National Council of the Episcopal Church (New York: National Council of the Episcopal Church, 1952), p. 6.
24. Ibid., pp. 13f.
25. Hooker, V.7.1–2.
26. Ibid., I.10.8.
27. Gordon R. Dunstan, *The Artifice of Ethics* (London: SCM Press, 1974), pp. 52f.
28. Kirk, *Conscience*, p. 103.
29. H. Richard Niebuhr, *Christ and Culture* (New York: Harper & Row, 1951), p. 19.
30. Dunstan, *Artifice*, p. 7.
31. Ibid., pp. 9, 14f.
32. Ibid., pp. 13f.
33. Maurice, *Kingdom*, II, p. 229.
34. Ibid., p. 231.
35. Ibid., p. 237.
36. Egil Grislis, "The Hermeneutical Problem in Hooker" in W. Speed Hill (ed.), *Studies in Richard Hooker* (Cleveland: Press of Case Western Reserve University, 1972), pp. 180ff.
37. Ibid. This is Grislis's own interpretation.
38. T. S. Eliot, "Thoughts After Lambeth" in Paul Elmen (ed.), *The Anglican Moral Choice* (Wilton, Conn.: Morehouse-Barlow Co., 1983), p. 118.
39. Kenneth Kirk, *Ignorance, Faith and Conformity* (London: Longmans, Green and Co., 1933), p. 148.
40. Basil Mitchell, *Law, Morality and Religion in a Secular Society* (New York: Oxford University Press, 1970), pp. 131ff.
41. Hooker, *Laws*, II.7.3.
42. Ibid., II.8.2–7.
43. Maurice, *Kingdom*, II, pp. 26f.
44. Ibid., p. 222. The true Christian rule, he continues, is "[N]ever resist evil for a selfish purpose. . . . [The Christian] does not say that he will not resist evil; for if he did, he would say that he would not be like his Lord, whose whole life on earth, and whose life in his members, is a constant resistance to evil. He determines not

to go to law to avenge himself, or get himself profit: he does not determine that he will not go to law, if the dignity of law be assailed by some illegal power" (pp. 224f.).

45. Dunstan, *Artifice*, p. 29.

46. Joseph Fletcher, *Morals and Medicine* (Boston: The Beacon Press, 1960), p. 218.

47. Ibid., p. 214.

48. Cf., e.g., ibid., pp. 61, 215f.

Chapter 2/Sharing

1. Marion J. Hatchett, *Commentary on the American Prayer Book* (New York: The Seabury Press, 1981), p. 366.

2. *The Book of Common Prayer and Administration of the Sacraments and Other Rites and Ceremonies of the Church Together with the Psalter or Psalms of David According to the Use of the Episcopal Church* (New York: Church Hymnal Corporation, 1979), p. 363. Emphasis added.

3. Charles Gore, *The Body of Christ* (London: John Murray, 1907), p. 25.

4. Ibid., p. 31.

5. Ibid., p. 203.

6. Ibid., pp. 206–209.

7. Ibid., p. 203.

8. *Book of Common Prayer*, p. 362.

9. Hatchett, *Commentary*, p. 374.

10. Lambourne, *Community*, p. 72.

11. For a discussion of political uses of the body metaphor, see John David Orens in Paul Elmen (ed.), *Anglican*.

12. Jeremy Taylor, *Holy Dying* iii, 3; quoted in Thomas Wood, *English Casuistical Divinity During the Seventeenth Century* (London: SPCK, 1952), p. 92.

13. Hooker, Preface III.

14. Hatchett, *Commentary*, pp. 345ff.

15. *Book of Common Prayer*, p. 360.

16. Michael Wilson, *The Church Is Healing* (London: SCM Press, 1966), p. 38.

17. Michael Wilson, *The Hospital—A Place of Truth: A Study of the Role of the Hospital Chaplain* (Birmingham, England: University of Birmingham Institute for the Study of Worship and Religious Architecture, 1971), p. 41.

18. Ibid., p. 72.

19. Ibid., p. 55. Robert A. Lambourne, "With Love to the USA" in M. A. H. Melinsky (ed.), *Religion*, 1:134; Robert A. Lambourne, "Towards an Understanding of Medico-Theological Dialogue" in M. A. H. Melinsky (ed.), *Religion*, 2:23.

20. John C. Fletcher, *Coping with Genetic Disorders* (San Francisco: Harper & Row, 1982), p. 84.

21. Lambourne, *Community*, p. 130.

22. Ibid., p. 131.

23. Joseph Fletcher, *Morals*, p. 62.

24. Gordon R. Dunstan, "Discerning the Duties" in Cicely M. Saunders (ed.), *The Management of Terminal Disease* (London: Edward Arnold, 1978), p. 185. Cf. T. S. West, "In-Patient Management of Advanced Malignant Disease," in Saunders, *Management*, p. 144.

25. Kirk, *Conscience*, pp. 346f.
26. See Dietrich Bonhoeffer, *Ethics* (New York: The Macmillan Co., 1962), pp. 326–34, and David Jenkins, "Good News and Bad News" in Melinsky, *Religion*, 1:102ff.
27. John Fletcher, *Coping*, pp. 34–41.
28. Ibid., pp. 105f.
29. Ibid., p. 56.
30. Ibid., p. 58.
31. Ibid., p. 63.
32. Ibid., p. 65.
33. Ibid., p. 83.
34. Cicely Saunders, "The Moment of Truth" in Leonard Pearson (ed.), *Death and Dying* (Cleveland: Press of Case Western Reserve University, 1969), p. 59.
35. Ibid., pp. 62f.
36. Wilson, *Hospital*, p. 44.
37. Michael Walzer, *Spheres of Justice* (New York: Basic Books, 1983), p. 76.
38. Ibid., p. 90.
39. Henry J. Aaron and William B. Schwartz, *The Painful Prescription: Rationing Hospital Care* (Washington, D. C.: The Brookings Institution, 1984), p. 134.
40. Brian Schrag, "Social Obligations for Primary Care," in David H. Smith (ed.), *Respect and Care in Medical Ethics* (Lanham, Md.: University Press of America, 1984).

Chapter 3/Mortality

1. Wilson, *Hospital*, p. 24.
2. Taylor, *Dying*, III, ii and viii.
3. Ibid., i.
4. Ibid., ii.
5. Ibid., "Epistle Dedicatory."
6. Ibid., III, iv.
7. Ibid., II, ii.
8. Ibid., III, viii.
9. Hooker, *Laws*, V.72.
10. Taylor, *Dying*, III, vi.
11. Wilson, *Hospital*, p. 121.
12. Lambourne, *Community*, p. 127.
13. *Book of Common Prayer*, p. 306.
14. Michael Wilson, *Health Is for People* (London: Darton, Longman and Todd, 1975), p. 76.
15. Wilson, *Hospital*, p. 118.
16. Wilson, *Church*, p. 91.
17. Lambourne, *Community*, p. 134.
18. Ibid., p. 140.
19. Taylor, *Dying*, V, iii. See Section v: Repentance is not to be deferred to the death bed. "A repentance upon our death bed is like washing the corpse, it is cleanly and civil, but makes no change deeper than the skin."

20. Ibid., iv.
21. Ibid., viii.
22. *Book of Common Prayer*, p. 507. Characteristically, details of what it means for an individual to be raised are not spelled out.
23. Taylor, *Dying*, V, viii.

Chapter 4/Decisions about Death

1. For a discussion of these issues along more traditional lines, see Waddams, *A New Introduction*, Chapters 4 and 5, and Lindsay Dewar, *An Outline of Anglican Moral Theology* (London: A. R. Mowbray and Co., 1968), Chapters 2 and 3. I think that the approach I develop in the text is consistent with traditional Anglican probabiliorism, but this is not the place to try to make that case. See Dunstan, *Artifice*, p. 91: "This 'principle of double-effect' is not popular among philosophers, chiefly, perhaps, because it can lend itself to specious abuse. But it is a principle with which we have to live in a world where absolute and unmingled good is not at our command."
2. Board for Social Responsibility (of Church of England), *On Dying Well: An Anglican Contribution to the Debate on Euthanasia* (London: Church Information Office, 1975), p. 9.
3. See Stanley Hauerwas, *Truthfulness and Tragedy* (Notre Dame: University of Notre Dame Press, 1977), pp. 101–16, and Gilbert Meilaender, "The Distinction Between Killing and Allowing to Die," *Theological Studies* 37 (September 1976): 467–70.
4. An earlier version of this section appears in Arthur Caplan and Thomas Murray (eds.), *Which Babies Shall Live?* (Clifton, N.J.: Humana Press, 1985).
5. Superior Court of New Jersey, *In the Matter of Karen Quinlan*, 137 N.J. Super. 227.
6. *Eichner v. Dillon*, 73 A.D. 2d 431, 426 N.Y.S. 2d 517 (1980).
7. Dunstan, *Artifice*, p. 91.
8. *Superintendent of Belchertown State School v. Saikewicz*, 373 Mass. 728, 370 N.E. 2d 417 (1977).
9. *In re Quinlan*, Supreme Court of New Jersey, A–116 (March 31, 1976).
10. Paul Ramsey, *The Patient as Person* (New Haven: Yale University Press, 1970), Chapter VI.
11. *On Dying Well*, p. 6.
12. Peter Baelz, "Voluntary Euthanasia," in *Theology* 75, no. 623 (May 1972): 248.
13. *On Dying Well*, p. 16.
14. Baelz, "Voluntary Euthanasia," p. 243.
15. Ibid., p. 247.
16. Taylor, *Dying*, IV, i.
17. Ibid., III, ix; cf. Hooker V.46.2.
18. Hugh Trowell, *The Unfinished Debate on Euthanasia* (London: SCM Press, 1973), pp. 121–31.
19. *On Dying Well*, p. 22.
20. Dunstan, *Artifice*, pp. 92f.

21. On the Samaritans, see Chad Varah (ed.), *The Samaritans* (New York: The Macmillan Co., 1965).

22. For a more detailed discussion of forms of medical care at the end of life, see Cicely Saunders (ed.), *The Management of Terminal Illness* (London: Arnold, 1978).

Chapter 5/Sexuality and New Life

1. *Book of Common Prayer*, p. 423.

2. Hatchett, *Commentary*, p. 432.

3. *Book of Common Prayer*, p. 425.

4. Hatchett, *Commentary*, p. 434.

5. Hooker, V.72.2.

6. On the history, see D. S. Bailey, *The Man-Woman Relation in Christian Thought* (London: Longmans, Green and Co., 1959).

7. Oliver O'Donovan, "Transsexualism and Christian Marriage," *Journal of Religious Ethics* 2, no. 1 (Spring 1983): 140. The argument is developed in *Begotten or Made?* (Oxford: Oxford University Press, 1984).

8. Ibid., p. 141.

9. Ibid., p. 145.

10. Ibid., pp. 150ff.

11. Ibid., p. 158.

12. (London: Longmans, Green and Co., 1955); reprinted by The Shoe String Press (Hamden, Conn.: Archon Books, 1975).

13. Norman Pittenger, "A Theological Approach to Understanding Homosexuality," in Ruth T. Barnhouse and Urban T. Holmes (eds.), *Male and Female* (New York: The Seabury Press, 1976), p. 165.

14. William Muehl, "Some Words of Caution" in Barnhouse and Holmes, *Male and Female*, p. 174.

15. For a strong argument for "equal status," see James B. Nelson, *Embodiment: An Approach to Sexuality and Christian Theology* (Minneapolis: Augsburg Publishing House, 1978), Chapter 8.

16. Ruth Tiffany Barnhouse, *Homosexuality* (New York: The Seabury Press, 1977), pp. 165–75.

17. Ibid., pp. 151f.

18. *Homosexual Relationships: A Contribution to Discussion* (London: Church Information Office, 1979).

19. Basil G. Mitchell, "The Homosexuality Report," *Theology* 83, no. 693 (May 1980): 189.

20. See *Book of Common Prayer*, p. 429.

21. Hatchett, *Commentary*, p. 446.

22. John Fletcher, *Coping*, p. 115.

23. Ibid., p. 110.

24. James M. Gustafson, *Theology and Christian Ethics* (Philadelphia: United Church Press, 1974), pp. 229–44, 273–86.

25. For a history of the controversy, see Harmon L. Smith, "Contraception and Natural Law: A Half-Century of Anglican Moral Reflection" in Elmen, *Anglican*,

pp. 181–200. An important document in that history in the Church of England is "The Family in Contemporary Society" in Ian T. Ramsey (ed.), *Christian Ethics and Contemporary Philosophy* (London: SCM Press, 1966), pp. 340–81.

26. Board for Social Responsibility (of Church of England), *Sterilization: An Ethical Inquiry* (London: Church Information Office, 1961), pp. 18–20.

27. Ibid., pp. 28–31.

28. See ibid., p. 128.

29. Ibid., pp. 40ff.

30. *The Blue Book: Reports of the Committees, Commissions, Boards, and Agencies of the General Convention of the Episcopal Church* (New Orleans: General Convention, 1982), p. 133.

31. Ibid., pp. 140–42.

32. Thus I side with the minority in the Canadian report on AID published as Phyllis Creighton, *Artificial Insemination by Donor* (Toronto: The Anglican Book Centre, 1977), particularly p. 62.

33. Paul F. Camenisch, "Abortion, Analysis and the Emergence of Value," *Journal of Religious Ethics* 4, no. 1 (Spring 1976): 131–58.

34. Throughout this section I am heavily dependent on the work of Leon Kass. Cf. "Making Babies Revisited," *The Public Interest* 54 (Winter 1979): 32–60. Reprinted in his *Toward a More Natural Science* (New York: The Free Press, 1985), esp. pp. 102–106, 110–15.

35. Dunstan, *Artifice*, p. 69.

36. Ibid., p. 71.

37. Board for Social Responsibility (of Church of England), *Abortion: An Ethical Discussion* (London: Church Information Office, 1965), pp. 31f.

38. Portions of this section appeared in David H. Smith and Linda Bernstein (eds.), *No Rush to Judgment* (Bloomington, Ind.: The Poynter Center, 1978), and are used here by permission of the Indiana University Foundation.

39. Board for Social Responsibility, *Abortion*, p. 20.

40. Judith Thomson, "A Defense of Abortion," in Joel Feinberg (ed.), *The Problem of Abortion* (Belmont, Calif.: Wadsworth, 1973), pp. 121–40.

41. *Hastings Studies* 2, no. 1 (January 1974).

42. See Daniel Callahan's discussion of the situation in the United Kingdom in *Abortion: Law, Choice and Morality* (New York: Macmillan, 1970), pp. 142–48, 284–304, and 486–92.

43. Dunstan, *Artifice*, p. 87.

44. Ibid., p. 88.

45. Callahan, chapter 8.

HEALTH/MEDICINE AND THE FAITH TRADITIONS

Advisory Board